THE BATTLE
OF THE
SPANISH ARMADA
1588

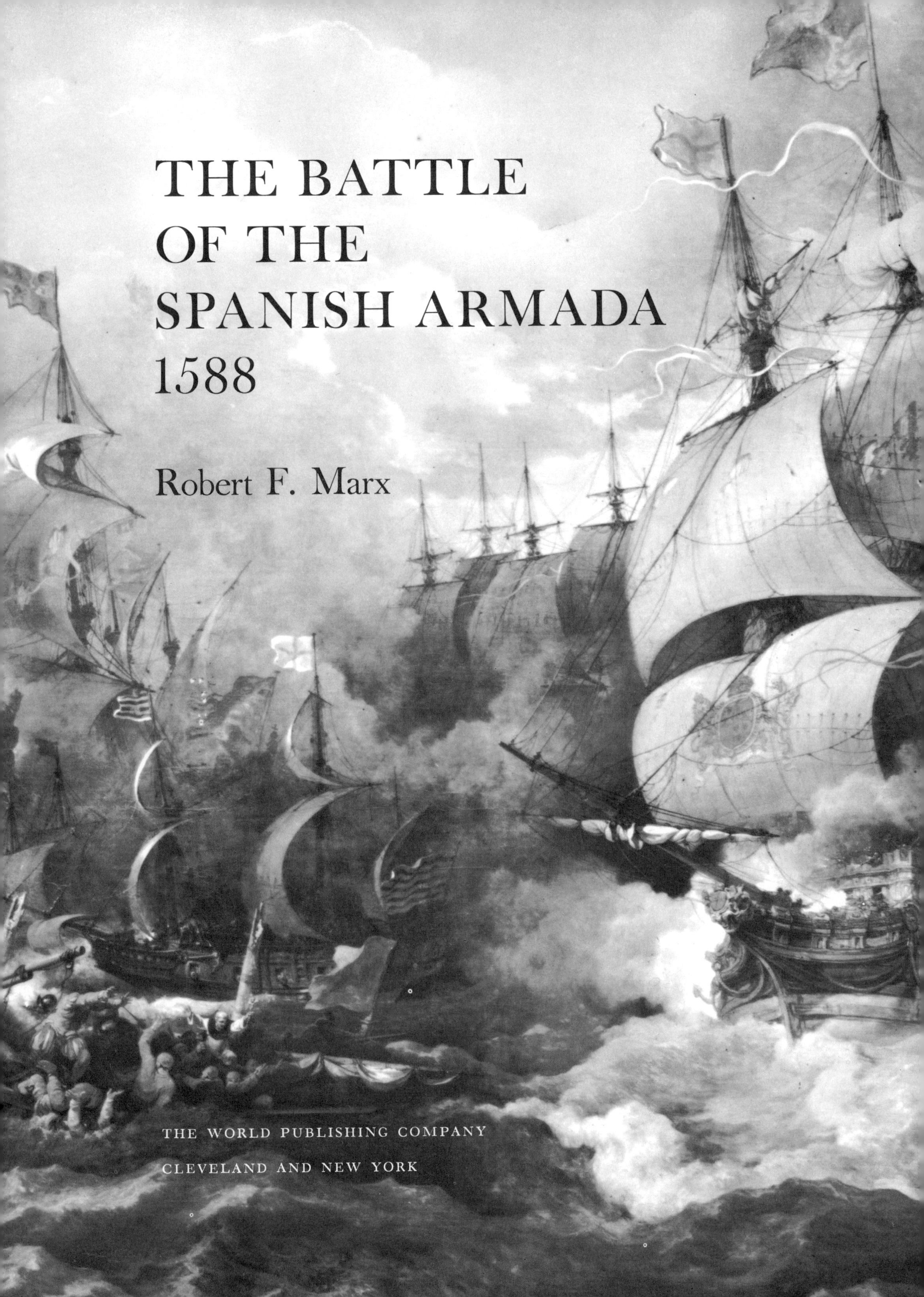

THE BATTLE OF THE SPANISH ARMADA
1588

Robert F. Marx

THE WORLD PUBLISHING COMPANY

CLEVELAND AND NEW YORK

Published by The World Publishing Company
2231 West 110th Street, Cleveland 2, Ohio
Published simultaneously in Canada by
Nelson, Foster & Scott Ltd.
Library of Congress Catalog Card Number: 65-19718
FIRST EDITION
CPWP

Designed by Jack Jaget

For Weezie, Skipper, Sibyl,
Kemp, Robert, and Christopher

THE BATTLE OF THE SPANISH ARMADA 1588

I

THE GREAT NAVAL BATTLE between Spain and England in 1588—one of the most important in the history of the world—is known as the Battle of the Invincible Armada. But in a sense this is the wrong name. An invincible armada is one that cannot be defeated, yet the mighty fleet of warships that Spain sent to invade England was defeated, so badly that Spain could never again rule the oceans. How was it possible that this armada, which had awed all Europe with its size and strength, was unable to stand up against the forces of a much smaller and less powerful enemy? The answer lies as much in the differences between these two countries and their rulers, Elizabeth I of England and Philip II of Spain, as in the actual battle that took place in the English Channel.

Spain in the sixteenth century was at the height of her power. At the end of the preceding century Columbus had discovered America, claiming it for the King and Queen of Spain. This vast New World which lay open to Spanish conquest and trade yielded great riches in gold, silver, and precious gems that were the envy of Spain's European neighbors. In the same year as Columbus' first voyage, 1492, Spain also drove out the last of the Moorish invaders after more than seven hundred years of struggle. By 1580 King Philip II, who already had many possessions in Europe besides Spain, and who had annexed the country of Portugal with all its territory in Asia, was master of over three fourths of the known world, an empire far greater than the Romans had ever dreamed of.

Philip's father, Emperor Charles V, had had a dream of uniting all Christian Europe against the bold Turks and Moors who menaced the

Philip II,
King of Spain

Christian nations from one end of the Mediterranean Sea to the other, but the Protestant Reformation split Christendom into two parts that were more interested in fighting each other than in uniting against the Moslems. Philip shared his father's dream, although with a different aim. The Turks, defeated in a decisive sea battle in 1571, were no longer a serious danger, and Philip turned his attention to fighting his Protestant neighbors. Devoutly religious, Philip was willing to use all the resources of his empire, his treasure from the New World, his powerful armies, and his huge fleet of warships for the one goal of reuniting Europe under the Catholic faith, even if he had to drain his own country of men and money to achieve it. If his Invincible Armada had, in fact, been victorious and he had been able to invade England, then his dream might have come true. The Protestant Queen Elizabeth would have been replaced with a Catholic ruler and the Catholic religion restored throughout Europe.

England was as different from Spain as night from day. She had no great wealth. In fact, her tax revenues were so small that often the British monarchs were forced to sell their jewels and land to buy food when the meager taxes were not collected on time. As for being powerful, she was considered not even close to it. There were only a few men in arms, and England's ships were almost all merchant ships equipped for trade but not for warfare. A small country, England held no foreign territory except for one or two ports on the continent that were alternately won and lost throughout the sixteenth century.

At home, the throne was not every secure either. The other parts of the kingdom—Scotland, Wales, and Ireland—were at times in open revolt against it, and the English themselves were divided. The majority of the people still clung to the old Catholic religion either secretly or in the open, while even the Protestant minority in power plotted among themselves. Worst of all, or so it was believed, was the fact that the throne was occupied by a mere woman, who could not possibly stand up to the warring factions within her kingdom, much less to her powerful enemy on the Spanish throne, Philip II. But they underestimated her. Where Philip was an idealist, Elizabeth was practical. Where he was willing to throw all his wealth into fighting battles and gaining territory, she always avoided war. Caring nothing for an empire or international glory, she quietly went about building up the internal strength of her country and her treasury and gaining the admiration and loyalty of her subjects.

Elizabeth I,
Queen of England

This "mere" woman was to go down in history as one of the most capable and beloved rulers England ever had, and as Philip's most crafty and exasperating foe. First he had tried to marry her, but she cleverly put him off for years, never actually refusing. Then he tried to stir up rebellion against her inside England. Finally, when this failed, he attempted to invade her country and depose her himself.

There were three reasons why Philip needed either to conquer England or gain her friendship. First, Philip was the leader of the Catholic movement to wipe out the new heresy of Protestantism. The longer Elizabeth stayed on the throne the more difficult this task became. She not only was the most important Protestant ruler but also provided the Protestants in northern Europe with support in their resistance against the Church of Rome. In addition, English Catholics were being persecuted more and more severely, mainly because Elizabeth feared that they were not loyal to her. For a long time Philip was forced to endure this because Spain and the other main Catholic country, France, were fighting each other, and Philip needed to keep England neutral. But alliances were never permanent in Europe; countries that were bitter enemies one day became close allies the next. In 1572 the French decided to join Spain in a Catholic alliance against the Protestants. The Pope had long been pressing Philip to overthrow the heretic English queen. Now, with French aid, Philip realized that his chance to rescue the English Catholics from persecution was at hand.

Pope Sixtus V

Lisbon, with the Portuguese East Indian treasure fleet

But religious differences were not the only reason for invading England. Philip also wished to repay Elizabeth for all the misery she had caused him. For two decades her privateers had been sacking Spanish cities in America, seizing Spanish treasure ships, and even daring to explore and lay claim to Spanish territory.

Soon after Columbus discovered America, the King of Spain and the King of Portugal had agreed to divide up the entire world, except for Europe, between themselves. Spain was to have the right to explore, colonize, and trade with almost all of North and South America, and Portugal was to have the same right in Africa and Asia. Whether this agreement was fair or not is beside the point. What is important is that Philip believed that he had exclusive claim to America and that any other European nation which even ventured into his territories was defying his legal rights and deserved to be punished.

Sir John Hawkins

All Europe soon learned of the immense riches that Spain and Portugal gained from their trade and colonies and, naturally, wished a share in them. During the first half of the sixteenth century the western Atlantic Ocean was really a Spanish lake, for rarely did any foreigner venture into those waters. But soon after 1550 first the French and then the English started to send explorers to seek a Northwest Passage to Asia, believing that they could reach China by sailing west instead of going all the way around Africa. It wasn't until many years later that people realized that North and South America were one solid body of land; there was no way through until the Panama Canal was cut in the twentieth century.

English seamen explored and mapped almost the entire coast of North America from the Carolinas to Hudson Bay in search of this passage, and then Sir Walter Raleigh decided that English settlers should found a colony. In 1584 he obtained permission from Queen Elizabeth to seek suitable land and establish a colony which would produce commodities England had obtained from Spain before the bad feeling between the two countries had interrupted trade. His settlement on Roanoke Island in what was then Virginia had to be abandoned after a few years, but it was still the first English colony in the New World, and a defiant challenge to Philip's claim of owning all the land in the Western Hemisphere.

Philip objected not only to foreign colonies in his territory, but also to any kind of contact with America, even friendly trade. The English

16

soon learned what kind of welcome the Spanish could prepare for unwanted visitors. John Hawkins made three trips to the West Indies in the 1560s to sell African slaves to the Spanish settlers. The first trip made him the wealthiest man in his home town of Plymouth; the second made him the wealthiest man in England. The third would have made him one of the wealthiest men in Europe, for the Spanish were willing to pay high prices for the labor they needed to mine gold and raise crops. But before he could set sail for England with his money chests full of American gold and silver, his ships were caught in a storm and he was forced to enter the harbor of Veracruz in Mexico to make repairs. By that time orders had arrived from the Spanish king that Hawkins was to be punished for trespassing in Spanish waters, and the deceitful officials, after greeting him as a welcome guest, captured his men and burned his ships. Hawkins managed to escape with a handful of sailors to reach England, but neither he nor his countrymen were to forget this act of treachery and welcomed any opportunity to repay the Spanish for it in the future.

Instead of frightening the English, this deed actually provoked them into making increasingly bolder voyages, no longer only for trade, but now for plunder. A young seaman who had been one of the few survivors with Hawkins, Francis Drake, was to achieve such success in his raids that the Spanish colonists all along the Caribbean coasts came to fear him like the Devil himself.

Sir Francis Drake

During the spring of 1572 Drake set sail from Plymouth, England, on a bold secret mission, the first in his campaign to take revenge for the murder of his companions in Veracruz and gain a share of the Spanish riches. After many months his friends gave him up for lost, but then suddenly, on Sunday morning in the fall of that same year, his ship dropped anchor in Plymouth Sound. The congregation left the church in the middle of the sermon to rush down to the waterside and hear what had happened. Drake had landed on the Isthmus of Panama, captured the mule trains bearing the bullion from the gold and silver mines in Peru, and escaped to his waiting ship with the best part of the treasure.

Five years later he set out to perform an even more daring feat, his famous voyage around the world. On the way, as he sailed down the coast of South America, around the southern tip and north again before setting out across the Pacific Ocean, he captured and destroyed Spanish ships, some of them right in the harbor of a fortified Spanish port, and took their rich cargoes. When he reached England after three years, he was not only the first Englishman to enter the Pacific and the first to circumnavigate the globe, but also the most hated and feared Englishman in America.

Hawkins and Drake were certainly the most famous and successful of Spain's enemies, but many other English pirates and privateers were also causing considerable damage to Spanish pride and Philip's pocketbook. Spain could no longer feel secure as the unchallenged master of the West Indies. Unable to prevent these raids on his settled territory, Philip could not keep the English from colonizing the still uninhabited North America either. Years of threats had not forced Elizabeth to promise to keep her subjects out of Spanish waters; now he learned that she actually helped to finance these pirates and in return received her share of the booty.

Dependent on treasure from the Indies to finance all his European wars, Philip had to make sure that England was conquered.

Strangely enough, although Philip was well aware of all the reasons he should invade England, he could not bring himself to act until all his advisers had exhausted themselves with arguments and until the English had become so bold that they carried their raids right into his own home ports in Spain. Philip was reluctant to act, not because he feared losing but because he knew the great expense of waging even a successful war.

This chest, full of treasure,
was found on one of the captured Armada ships.

His armies were the most powerful in the world, but paying for them kept him almost bankrupt.

At first he hoped to solve the English problem by stirring up a revolution inside England that would not involve his soldiers. He began by smuggling into England hundreds of exiled priests of the newly founded Jesuit order to persuade the English Catholics to rise up against their heretic queen. But the English, even most of the Catholics, were too loyal to the popular Elizabeth, and her ministers were too vigilant. Nearly all of the Jesuits were arrested and either deported or executed for treason. In Ireland, Philip's troublemakers were also at work, and at first with more success. The Irish disliked English rule anyway, and the majority of the people had remained strong Catholics. In 1579 Philip and the Pope sent money and eventually a force of Spanish and Italian soldiers to aid the Irish to rebel, but after a brief period of victory they were all defeated. Elizabeth's forces executed every captured invader or rebel.

19

War was never formally declared between Spain and England, but by 1580, the year Drake returned from his famous voyage, Philip was convinced that internal rebellion would never succeed without the aid of a large Spanish army. For many years he had been considering the idea of an invasion of England—in fact, as early as 1563 military leaders had presented long and detailed plans for such an undertaking. However, two decades were to pass until Philip finally gave his approval to this daring scheme.

The real beginning of the Spanish Armada, the fleet of warships which was necessary for the invasion, was in 1583. The Spanish Navy, led by a brilliant officer who came from a long line of Spanish seamen, the Marquis of Santa Cruz, was then in splendid condition. In June of that year the Spanish fleet, under his command, won an overwhelming victory over a French Protestant fleet twice its size. This confirmed the impression made earlier by the Battle of Lepanto against the Turks, that Spanish fleets were as invincible on sea as Spanish armies were on land. Santa Cruz and other naval commanders were eager to follow this victory with another against the English in revenge for the many insults suffered at the hands of the English pirates.

For several years Santa Cruz had been thinking of an invasion of England. His main confederate was the Duke of Guise, who led The Catholic League in France. Their plan of action had been secretly arranged even before the Spanish naval victory in 1583.

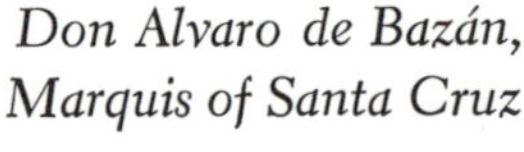

Don Alvaro de Bazán,
Marquis of Santa Cruz

The Duke of Guise was to cross the English Channel, under the protection of Santa Cruz and his fleet, and land an army in Sussex in the southeast of England. They would help the English Catholics to rebel, set the Catholic Mary Queen of Scots free and crown her Queen of England after killing Elizabeth. The fleet was ready, the French were ready; only Philip's consent was needed.

Santa Cruz was a rough old sailor who spoke his mind plainly even to his king. Like most of his countrymen, he was tired of seeing his master hesitate and let Elizabeth and her heathen pirates provoke Spain and go unpunished. Immediately after his great naval victory, Santa Cruz reported to Philip. Much to his dismay, Philip did not even reply to his suggestion that his fleet serve as the nucleus of a force for invading England. Two months later he tried again. In a strongly worded letter he begged the king to approve his plan of invasion immediately. Philip neither agreed nor refused. He thanked the admiral for his zeal, but said he must wait a little and watch.

One of the main reasons Philip hesitated was the enormous cost of preparing the fleet. He was horrified by the figure named by Santa Cruz—four million ducats. The armada that finally sailed in 1588 was to cost Philip over ten million ducats, and a ducat today would be worth about $12.50.

Philip ordered his most trusted counselors and military advisers to form a special council to draw up new plans. For the next two years the council reported nearly every day to the king with the latest advice on the situation and with new plans for his approval, but still Philip was reluctant to take the great risk. His waiting and uncertainty gave Elizabeth, who had many spies all over Europe, time to discover what was being planned for her and in reply she sent Francis Drake to do more mischief against the Spaniards.

This time Drake did not sail as a mere privateer but was openly commissioned by the queen to strike against Philip's possessions whenever and however he could. John Hawkins had been urging the queen to permit him to attack Spanish ports and intercept returning treasure fleets, but he was kept at home to build up a navy for England's defense and this dangerous mission was entrusted to Drake instead. So great was her faith in his ability that Elizabeth contributed a large sum of money out of her own treasury and two ships for the venture. Drake was fortunate

Martin Frobisher

to have as second-in-command his old friend and one of England's most experienced seamen, Martin Frobisher. Frobisher, like Drake and Hawkins, was from the same Plymouth area and was to gain great fame along with them in the Battle of the Spanish Armada in 1588.

Setting sail in September 1585, Drake and his twenty-nine ships made for northern Spain, where all they accomplished was to learn the sad news that the treasure fleets had already arrived safely in their home ports in the south, and thus there was no chance for the English to capture them. But Drake was determined not to return empty-handed, and set off for the West Indies in search of booty. All the way there and back, disaster alternated with success. His crew came down with fever after stopping in the Cape Verde Islands off the coast of Africa, but with fair weather he was able to cross the Atlantic and reach a small uninhabited island in the Caribbean Sea where the sick could be nursed back to health and preparations made for the boldest English attacks to date.

At sunrise on New Year's Day of 1586 the unsuspecting inhabitants of Santo Domingo, the oldest Spanish city in America, awoke to find Drake's fleet anchored in their harbor. Unaware that most of the English had gone ashore during the night, the Spanish sent the entire garrison of the fort to meet a small landing force that Drake used as a decoy. As soon as the soldiers and most of the menfolk of the city had run out to the beach, Drake gave the signal, the hidden English sailors rushed forward, and the astonished Spaniards surrendered with scarcely a struggle.

The city's capture was a great blow to Spanish pride but a disappointment to the English in search of booty. Several cannon, a few small ships, and a little ransom money for wealthy hostages were all they gained. Drake decided to head directly to the richest and strongest port on the Spanish Main, the great city of Cartagena. Supposedly safe from attack because it was entirely surrounded by sea or marshes, Cartagena also had a huge garrison of soldiers, who by the time Drake arrived had already been warned and had spent a full month preparing for him. Once again he outsmarted the Spaniards by landing at night, this time entering the city from the rear where no one expected him. After a brief clash of arms the defenders fled before the small band of English. But the victors were to suffer a worse defeat. Another epidemic of fever broke out among Drake's men, who suffered much more than the local people, used to this type of illness. Drake was forced to abandon his plan of leaving a permanent force behind to hold the city as an English possession, and to leave the Indies without plundering any more ports, except Saint Augustine in Florida, or capturing richly laden galleons. He limped back to England with barely enough crew to man his ships and arrived in July 1586 to learn that news of his attacks had reached Spain and caused her to begin to outfit an armada of warships for an invasion of England.

The damage to Spain was much greater than one would think. Although Drake had not captured as much treasure as he had on his two earlier voyages, Philip's credit with his European bankers was shaken. Despite his enormous income, Philip was always in debt. He spent so much money on wars that he constantly had to borrow from the bankers and then repay them at high interest rates, when the treasure ships arrived. When the bankers feared the ships would not return, they would not lend him money, so that for lack of money to pay the troops, his wars were checked at a crucial moment. Every place Drake visited, he demolished the forts and removed the artillery. Restoring them and replacing captured ships would cost the almost bankrupt Philip huge sums of money he could not afford.

The Marquis of Santa Cruz and the other Spanish leaders could not help admiring the daring of the English pirates and the genius of the English queen, who acted while their king seemed asleep. Santa Cruz tried constantly to force Philip to strike back, appealing many times to his pride. He told Philip plainly that Elizabeth was making a fool of him and that the world was secretly laughing at the ease with which the English stole his money and wrecked his property. The longer Philip hesitated, the more powerful and bold England would become, and it might soon be impossible to defeat her.

Pride, loss of his wealth, and even devotion to his Catholic faith might never have decided Philip to take the fateful step, but to these reasons was added another danger, the risk of losing his possessions right in Europe. The Low Countries, as the modern nations of Holland and Belgium and parts of northern France were then called, were the most precious jewels in the Spanish crown. They were certainly the richest area in Europe at the time. Although their natural resources were limited, the people were so industrious and clever that they were considered the best traders and manufacturers in the world.

The trouble began in 1559 shortly after Philip, who as crown prince had been governing the Netherlands very ably for some years, left for Spain to be crowned king. The rule of these possessions was left in the hands of dishonest officials who were more interested in amassing fortunes quickly than in governing Philip's subjects well. Religion was another serious problem. As the Protestant Reformation gained more and more supporters each day, Philip's officials became increasingly cruel in persecuting them. Soon most of the Netherlands was in open revolt against Spain in a fierce struggle that was to last for over eighty years until the Dutch finally won their independence from Spain. Philip sent his ablest leaders there and poured millions of ducats into pursuing the war, but even though they won one battle after another, they could not defeat the hardy rebels entirely, mainly because they were receiving constant aid from other Protestant countries.

Elizabeth of England offended him the most. She was interested in helping the Dutch, not only out of sympathy with their religious grievances but also because she knew that as soon as Philip had crushed this rebellion he would send his entire army against her. There are many examples of how Elizabeth was able to frustrate Philip's plans with timely aid of money or soldiers to the rebels, and it is no wonder that he finally became determined to overthrow this cleverly meddlesome woman.

In 1578 Philip entrusted the war to the most famous military genius

Alessandro Farnese,
Duke of Parma

of his day, the thirty-three-year-old Duke of Parma. When he arrived the duke found that William of Orange, the leader of the rebels, was everywhere victorious, but the duke soon proved more than a match for his rival. First he took advantage of the many divisions in the ranks of William's supporters, especially between the Dutch, the Flemings, and the Walloons from the southern part of the Low Countries. By skillful persuasion and bribery he soon brought the Catholic Walloon provinces back under Spanish rule. The seven northern provinces, which today form the country of Holland, were predominantly Protestant and joined even more closely in an effort to preserve their independence from Spain.

Parma was an excellent soldier as well as an able diplomat, and he was gradually able to retake more and more of the rebel strongholds. His greatest feat was the capture of the Flemish city of Antwerp, which was then the most important city in the Netherlands, in August 1585. Finding it strongly defended by a resolute garrison and almost surrounded by water, which made a siege more difficult, he had first cut off all access between the city and the sea by means of a bridge of boats. Then he waited patiently until the defenders, who were unable to bring in food from the outside, were finally forced to surrender or starve to death.

By this time it seemed to the Spanish as if the rebellion would soon be over, especially after its leader, William of Orange, was assassinated in 1584. But they had forgotten Elizabeth, who realized that as soon as the

The bridge of boats built by the Duke of Parma during siege of Antwerp

last shot had been fired in Holland, the Duke of Parma and his powerful
army might be sent across the Channel to invade England. She was also
particularly furious with Philip at that time. During the preceding three
years over twenty attempts on her life had been planned, and each time
only the vigilance of her ministers, who had many spies, had saved her
from death. She was sure that Philip was secretly behind all these plots.
In fact, in one case the Spanish ambassador had been caught in the act
of bribing someone to assassinate her and had been promptly expelled
from England.

So Elizabeth decided to pay Philip back by helping the rebels in the
Netherlands. Although she sent only a small force of 5000 infantrymen
and 1000 cavalrymen under the Earl of Leicester, plus a substantial sum
of money and war material, nevertheless this was enough to sustain them
until the son of William of Orange, Maurice of Nassau, was able to take
command and renew the struggle with vigor. In fact, her action was one
of the most important contributions to Dutch independence, which was

finally won in 1648 when Spain agreed to set the Netherlands free. To this day the Dutch still feel grateful to the English for that help. And for the same reason, Philip was enraged. England had been giving unofficial aid for two decades, but this open league with the rebels was the last straw that finally overcame Philip's hesitation. He had been cautious too long. Within an hour after he had received the news that Elizabeth's small army had landed, he ordered his admiral, Santa Cruz, to draw up new and final plans for the invasion of England.

Philip decided that, instead of using the land forces that the French Duke of Guise had offered, he would send his own army from the Netherlands. All of his spies in England and on the continent agreed that the most Elizabeth would be able to raise in defense of her throne was an ill-equipped and undisciplined rabble, nothing capable of repelling a powerful, veteran army such as Parma's. Thus the conquest of England would be a matter of a few weeks at the most. Then Parma could quickly return to Holland and finish off the rebels without any interference from outside. The only weakness of the scheme lay in the difficulty of ferrying Parma's army, as well as all its supplies and war materials, across the Channel to English soil. Santa Cruz was placed in charge of planning all naval aspects of the invasion, the preparation of an invincible armada to carry an invincible army.

The scene was finally set!

English forces landing on Dutch soil, 1585

THE MARQUIS OF SANTA CRUZ set about his task in great haste, but it took him nearly three months to complete the drafting of such important plans, leaving him exhausted but still an enthusiastic supporter of the invasion. If he had known that before the Armada finally sailed Philip would make so many drastic changes in his original plans, he might not have been so careful and taken so long in their preparation.

During this same period Philip was, as always, extremely busy too. One of his greatest fears was that the preparations for the invasion might force him to cancel one of his annual treasure fleets, cutting off his only real source of revenue at a time when he needed money more than ever. His

Lisbon

first task then was to make the treasure fleets independent of the Armada so that they could continue on their regular, vitally important schedules. Even though one could say that Philip was the richest monarch in the world, the truth was that he was perpetually in debt and no sooner did a treasure fleet reach the port of Seville than all its cargo was sent off again to repay his creditors. Poor Philip barely had possession of it for a few days. Fully aware that he was embarking on the most expensive venture of his career, he naturally worried how he could raise all the money he needed for it.

Philip believed that since the Catholic Church had so much to gain from the conquest of England, the Pope should help with the great expense of this venture. He claimed that the invasion was to be undertaken primarily for the purpose of restoring the Catholic faith in England, but the Pope, Sixtus V, was inclined to view the matter in a different light. He knew that the religious question was only one of several reasons why Philip wished to conquer England, and he knew too that if the attempt were successful, Spain would gain much more than Rome. Also he realized that Philip, already a stubborn and independent-minded ruler, would become even more powerful and more difficult for him to handle.

For several years the Spanish ambassador in Rome had tried to extort a sizable contribution for the invasion from the Pope, but all he had been able to gain was promises. On the very day that Philip had ordered Santa Cruz to begin making plans for the Armada, he wrote directly to the Pope,

*Armada playing card
showing the Pope contributing
"a million of gold"*

instead of through his ambassador, demanding in plain words that the Pope immediately show his wholehearted support of the venture, and prove it by making a large donation. On Christmas Eve, Philip received a generous Christmas gift from the Pope. Sitting in his cold, dark palace, the Escorial, outside Madrid, Philip learned that the Pope had agreed to meet all his demands and had granted him for seven years all the revenues received from the Church in Spain, amounting annually to 1,800,000 crowns, a very substantial sum indeed. Besides this subsidy he would send Philip a bonus of 1,000,000 crowns the very instant he learned that the Spanish invading army had set foot on English soil. Philip was also busy negotiating with foreign bankers, mostly in Venice and Genoa, for large loans.

Early in January 1586, without even waiting for Santa Cruz to finish his Armada plans, Philip ordered the Duke of Parma in the Low Countries to begin building the vessels needed to ferry his army across the Channel to England, and to amass all the supplies of ammunition and weapons necessary for fighting the English. Meanwhile Santa Cruz, who believed Parma's invasion force should sail from Spain with the Armada, labored diligently over the details of creating, outfitting, paying and carrying this army. Santa Cruz took months to finish his plans. Early in March he sent Philip a copy of the preliminary estimates. Gigantic in size, careful down to the smallest detail, the report was appalling to Philip, who could only think of how to prepare a successful invasion without going completely bankrupt.

Santa Cruz had demanded 556 ships, 40 small boats to be used for carrying messages and scouting ahead of the main fleet, and 200 flat-bottomed barges to carry the army he still expected to bring from Spain for the invasion. Of the 556 ships, only a little over a third were to be fighting ships; the rest were troop transports and supply boats. The fleet was to carry about 100,000 men, over half of whom were soldiers. Finding food and drink for nearly 100,000 mouths for a voyage that would last at least six months into waters where new supplies could not be obtained was an almost impossible task. The list of provisions the admiral submitted seemed unbelievable. To name but a few items: biscuit, almost 40,000,000 pounds; bacon, 2,280,000 pounds; beans and rice, 66,000 bushels; cheese, 2,150,000 pounds; wine (to kill the taste of the food), 5,148,000 gallons; water, 2,200,000 gallons; and fodder for the 1600 horses and 1400 mules which the Armada would also carry for the invasion.

There is no doubt that the first item the frugal king looked for was the total cost of the enterprise. Excluding the actual value of the vessels needed, the figure was staggering: 3,801,233 ducats, of which less than half was to be levied in Philip's Italian and other Mediterranean possessions; the rest was to be raised in Spain. Santa Cruz did mention that it would no doubt turn out to be somewhat less expensive than that, because he had included the salaries for each soldier and sailor involved for a period of eight months, and certainly many would be killed in battle, others desert, and some die of natural causes.

With only one great modification—that of using Parma's army instead of taking the invasion force from Spain—Philip approved the plan but on a much smaller scale, for he realized the impossibility of supplying all the items Santa Cruz asked for.

Immediately there were signs of great activity in all the ports and shipyards of Spain, Portugal, and Spanish Italy. Philip had already taken steps to increase the size of his navy by committing another act of treachery against the English. He ordered his officials to seize all English vessels found in his ports and turn them over to his admirals. All the crews from the forty or so ships that were taken were forced to serve in his galleys as slaves. When news of this horrible deed reached England, the infuriated English attacked the only two Spanish ships in England at that time and

Portuguese carracks

nearly tore the poor crews to pieces before bailiffs could restrain them and rescue the Spaniards.

All over Europe, Philip's agents began buying the countless items necessary to outfit such a fleet. Elsewhere recruiters were raising crews to man the ships that were being built and bought and soldiers to defend the fleet.

Philip also sent out strict orders that the purpose of all these preparations was to be kept secret. Rumors were deliberately spread that an armada was being prepared for some vast project of conquest in America. Sometimes hints were dropped by Philip's ambassadors in foreign courts that Spain was sending a fleet to crush the rebellion in the Netherlands. To keep Elizabeth off guard, Philip and the Duke of Parma both wrote her sweet letters declaring falsely that their only desire was to have peace with England.

However, Elizabeth could not look upon the gathering of such a force without suspecting that it might be used against her, and it did not take her spies long to discover that the real plan was to invade and conquer England. But hating war, she was reluctant to believe this or to make preparations to meet the threat. Only after constant urging by her ministers did she finally decide to mobilize one fifth of her navy and place the rest on alert.

News of Sir Francis Drake's success in the West Indies reached England before he did, and to complete his work Elizabeth's ministers advised her to send a fleet out to intercept Philip's returning treasure fleets and the Portuguese carracks bringing back rich cargoes of spices and silks from the East Indies. All of this vitally important shipping was expected to approach the Spanish coast in the late summer by way of the Azores, a group of islands about 650 miles west of Portugal. When John Hawkins had returned from his last slave-trading voyage to the Indies he had been given the task of rebuilding and increasing the size of Elizabeth's navy, which he had undertaken with great enthusiasm and skill. For years he had been begging the queen for a chance to take revenge on the Spaniards for the murder of his crew in Veracruz; realizing that she had restrained him for so long unjustly while Drake had been given many chances to attack the Spanish, she chose Hawkins for this new venture. She gave him four of the best 500-ton galleons of her navy, so that, counting the other vessels given by London merchants, his fleet totaled eighteen when he set sail the last week in August, 1586.

His voyage was to be a very short one indeed. Only a few days later a ship from home overtook him with orders from the queen to return to English waters and sail up and down the Channel guarding the coasts. On the same day that Hawkins had sailed, English Catholics had started rioting all over England, and countless rumors were heard that French forces, under the leadership of the Duke of Guise, were going to attempt a landing in Sussex to join the Catholics in overthrowing Elizabeth. Later, when it was learned that the riots were not on a large scale and that there was no real danger of an invasion from France, many believed that the trouble had been started by Philip's agents for the express purpose of stopping Hawkins' fleet. If this is true then they were very clever, for Elizabeth kept Hawkins cruising in those waters for over three weeks, until it was certain that the danger was over.

Only then did he receive orders to continue with his original mission, but by then it was too late. Reaching the Azores, he learned that he had already missed the Portuguese carracks carrying treasure from the East Indies, and the treasure fleet from the West Indies, with the exception of one straggler, which he captured. The rest of the cruise yielded only isolated prizes of little value. By the end of October his fleet was back in England, having inflicted only minimal damage to Spain's plans.

Meanwhile the Armada preparations were progressing at a very slow pace, which caused Philip and his advisers a great deal of worry. He was forced to decrease the size of the fleet nearly daily, because of the impossibility of obtaining all that was needed for the huge force originally planned. Although Spain had one of the largest naval forces in the world, it also had many commitments, particularly the annual treasure fleets which required many warships to guard them from pirates. By the end of 1586 it appeared that it would take countless years longer to complete the preparations unless something drastic were done. So Philip decided to buy and lease vessels from German and Dutch Protestants, even though the owners of the ships knew by that time of their intended use against their ally England.

Philip's practice of making even the smallest decisions himself, coupled with the slowness of communications over such vast distances, slowed the preparations even more. Santa Cruz was forever writing Philip to change his mind and have the invasion force carried on the Armada vessels, as he had suggested from the start, but this insistence only annoyed the king, who was certain that his plan was more practical and more certain of success. Parma also was against Santa Cruz's plan. From a military viewpoint he knew that Philip was wrong. If his whole army were taken across to England, the rebels in the Netherlands could seize all the places it had taken him years to recapture, and also occupy the ports on the continent that would be needed in case of retreat. Yet the duke was a vain man and had no intention of waiting in the Netherlands while Santa Cruz gained all the fame and glory, so he enthusiastically agreed with Philip's plan of using his army and was made commander-in-chief of the invasion force.

Ultimately Philip was to pay heavily for this blunder, which was to cause the failure of the whole undertaking. Neither Philip nor his advisers knew enough of naval matters to realize the difficulty of getting a fleet, especially one driven only by sails, to turn up at exactly the right time and place. More than two centuries later the emperor Napoleon was to be guilty of a similar miscalculation, with similar results. The main difficulty lies in coordinating the two forces, land and sea, so that the one meets the other on time. In this case Parma had a relatively easy journey to make, only down to the Flemish ports. The Armada's task was much harder. It had to sail over hundreds of miles of water dominated by a watchful and determined enemy, to sweep the seas free of enemy ships

Queen Elizabeth preparing for invasion

The English Army at Tilbury

so that they could not interfere with the embarking of the invasion force, to carry this force across the Channel against the prevailing winds, and finally to land the army when probably every vessel in England, down to the smallest rowboat, would be out trying to prevent this landing. Santa Cruz's plan might have failed also, but at least it was not doomed from the start with this one great flaw.

Back in England, one of Elizabeth's major problems was the many contradictory reports she received on the state of the Spanish preparations. Some claimed that the Armada would never sail; others reported that it was already under sail, heading for England. She was sufficiently convinced of the danger to do something, but not enough so to mobilize her whole fleet. She ordered Sir Francis Drake to prepare a squadron to be provided with a landing force of soldiers for a great project financed by Elizabeth herself, Drake, and several London merchant bankers. Drake's instructions were to prevent the Spanish ships, then scattered in several ports, from uniting in the one great Armada, or to follow and attack them if they were already on their way toward England. He was also ordered to capture the Portuguese East Indian carracks and the Spanish West Indian treasure fleets and, if the opportunity arose, to enter the ports where the ships were preparing and destroy them. On second thought the queen decided that the last order was too risky and sent word to revoke it, but Drake had already sailed from Plymouth and the word never reached him.

Drake had had a premonition that the queen would cancel the whole expedition at the last moment as she had done with Hawkins, so he left port the moment the sailing orders arrived, on April 2, 1587, even without all the necessary water and food. His squadron was composed of twenty-three ships carrying 2200 men, the strongest fleet Elizabeth had ever sent to sea up to that time. Drake realized that the fate of England rested on him and he was intent on doing his utmost for his beloved country.

With a fair wind his squadron sighted Cape Finisterre in northern Spain three days out of port, but there a gale struck which scattered his ships in many directions and they could not reassemble until the sixteenth of April, right off Lisbon, the capital of Portugal. Santa Cruz was in Lisbon then overseeing the Armada preparations, but Drake, learning that there was an even greater concentration of ships at Cádiz, decided to attack there first.

Many of the Spanish ports, as they learned of Drake's approach, grew very uneasy, for his boldness and past successes were well known. But there was one place in Spain that did not fear him at all—Cádiz, the principal naval port, ringed with fortresses and castles. There lay the biggest galley fleet in the world, a fleet similar to that which had won the Battle of Lepanto against the Turks, a fleet that yearned to match its guns and rams with the insolent armed merchantmen of Drake.

Drake had no intention of disappointing them. Always bold beyond his strength and always ready for a challenge with great risks, he made straight for Cádiz and prepared to fight the dragon in the dragon's own cave. On the nineteenth of April he was off Cádiz with his four largest vessels, the others straggling behind. He wanted to take advantage of the element of surprise, for the Spaniards had not heard that he was heading that way, and he decided to enter port at once without waiting for the rest of the squadron. He called a council of war on his ship of the officers from the other three ships. His second-in-command protested vigorously that it was unwise to dash into Cádiz without waiting for the other vessels and without careful preparations, but Drake had already made up his mind on the matter and his opinion prevailed.

To appreciate Drake's famous attack on Cádiz it is necessary to under-

Spanish ships assembling at Lisbon

stand what types of vessels were involved, as well as a little about naval warfare until that time.

For many centuries up to and including 1571, the year of the Battle of Lepanto, the fighting navy of Spain, like that of any other Mediterranean power, had consisted almost entirely of galleys, those warships of ancient design propelled in battle by heavy oars called sweeps. Such craft had clashed with their rivals in the great inland sea, where conditions were ideal for them, long before the Romans. During all that time they had been the only warships, and they were to be used there for several centuries longer, but not on the same scale.

Sailing ships existed of course. Saint Paul had been shipwrecked in one fifteen centuries before Lepanto, but they were for trade, not war. Northern Europeans were the first to realize that galleys were not suitable for the big waves and fierce storms of the Atlantic Ocean, and as early as the fourteenth century they began to replace their galley-style vessels with another type more suitable to their seas. During the age of early

37

English man-of-war 1588

explorations and discoveries, Spain and other maritime powers of the Mediterranean also realized that the galleys were unsuitable for long ocean voyages, and like their northern neighbors began to build vessels with larger hulls. These were propelled by sails, instead of by sweeps manned by slaves. As Spain started to trade with the New World, it had to build even better vessels than those small ones used for explorations and coastal trading around Europe. This was the birth of the large galleon type of vessel that is called by so many different names, depending on its size and use. Basically it was built with a round bottom for better safety in storms, huge holds for cargo, very high sides to keep out heavy seas, and several masts to carry plenty of sail. These vessels were lightly armed with a few pieces of artillery, but naval leaders in Spain were reluctant to think of them as warships, mainly because of their clumsy appearance and slow speed. They preferred the swift galleys, which could move in any direction no matter which way the wind blew, and which had always before proved so effective in battle.

The English, mainly due to men like Hawkins and Drake, had more foresight and saw that galleons had better fighting qualities than the Spaniards realized. They began with the basic design of the Spanish galleons but built them on much lighter lines, not trying to get maximum cargo space, and arming them with a great number of heavy artillery pieces. The Spaniards of course knew of the newly designed ships the

English were producing, but never put much stock in them. Santa Cruz proposed using many galleons in the Armada, but mainly because they could carry larger numbers of soldiers than could the galleys.

Sea fighting up until this time had been chiefly a matter of firing a few pieces of artillery to frighten the enemy and then boarding their ships quickly with soldiers. This softening-up process rarely lasted over a few minutes, usually only until the attacker could bring his ship alongside the enemy ship, seize it, and hold fast to it with grappling hooks and lines in such a way that the soldiers could leap aboard the enemy vessel at the lowest part, the waist or middle. During the last stages of the approach before the vessels were joined together, archers and gunmen in the upper decks and rigging shot at the defenders on the enemy ship to keep them scattered and under cover. Then the soldiers would board and overpower any resistance.

At the time when Drake was nearing Cádiz there were about eighty ships there, both large and small. Most of these were destined for service in the Armada; the others were being fitted out for that year's treasure fleets. To guard the port there was a very strong squadron of twelve royal galleys, but unfortunately for the Spaniards these galleys were the only vessels in condition to fight. Few of the others had received their guns or seagoing crews yet, and many of the impressed merchantmen had even had their sails removed to prevent their escaping. However, the fortifications were strongly manned and gunned, and an attack on Cádiz would have been considered sheer suicide even if the galleys had not been there. Drake had learned much concerning these conditions from neutral vessels which he had stopped and questioned as he sailed for Cádiz.

The royal galleys, with trumpets blaring and decorated with a great array of brilliantly colored flags and pennants, came rowing out to meet Drake, not really certain that he was an enemy until he finally raised the English flag at the last minute. The action that followed at the mouth of the great bay was to revolutionize naval warfare and to teach Philip and his navy a lesson they never forgot. Each of Drake's four galleons carried between thirty and thirty-five large pieces of artillery, while the galleys had only five each and these much smaller. Following their usual strategy, the commanders of the galleys planned to attack rapidly, ram the galleons with their knifelike prows, then board the doomed ships and slaughter the heretics.

Drake anticipated this maneuver and never gave the Spaniards the chance to carry out their plan. Opening up with all his artillery from each galleon, he crushed the approaching galleys with better-aimed and heavier fire. One galley was beached to prevent it from sinking and all the others fled, with heavy damages, to the protection of the shore batteries. Of the Spanish ships anchored off the town farther inside the bay, a few escaped into a small inner harbor, while smaller ones fled up various creeks. Those that could not be moved in time were quickly boarded by Drake's men, reinforced by the rest of his fleet which began to arrive on the scene, and were set on fire. This work went on well after nightfall, with the shore batteries firing into the smoke and flames, causing more damage to their own ships than to the English.

From several prisoners Drake learned that a huge galleon, owned personally by the Marquis of Santa Cruz and the one he planned to use as his flagship in the great Armada, was also in the inner harbor, believed by most Spaniards and almost all foreigners to be completely safe from attack. Drake had his own ideas about this and was determined to destroy that galleon. He moved his whole fleet, again over the protests of his second-in-command, to the entrance of the inner harbor, but still out of range of the fort guns, and in the morning led a flotilla of small craft to the attack. The great galleon, helpless for lack of guns, was quickly in flames. Although the Spaniards sent out their hastily patched-up galleys and let loose several fireships against Drake's fleet, all missed their mark.

Meanwhile Spanish soldiers ashore were busy bringing up field guns along the beach, and at noon, seeing that he had destroyed everything within reach, Drake decided it was time to leave. However, as suddenly as his decision was made the wind died down completely. For the next fourteen hours his fleet remained exposed to all the fire from the shore batteries, which he returned with such accuracy that he caused more damage than he suffered.

Early the next morning a land breeze rose and out the happy victors sailed, only to anchor just clear of Cádiz for another day while they sorted out the booty, made minor repairs, regrouped the fleet, and had the opportunity to beat off yet another determined galley attack. The galley commanders had certainly done their duty but the result was only to prove that these famous vessels were now obsolete.

When the news of this catastrophe was brought to Philip he raised

King Philip II, a painting by Rubens

his shaking hand with a nervous gesture, and for a long time stroked his chin uneasily, too stunned to speak. Heartless observers said that Drake had "singed His Majesty's beard," a phrase that was used for centuries afterward every time the English made mischief for Spain. Drake had taught Philip that some four fifths of his battle fleet was useless for the assault on England. Philip understood the lesson at once and made a revolutionary decision, not to use his galley fleet in the Armada at all. At this point he should have called off the whole venture, and most of his ministers even recommended such a move, but Philip felt too deeply committed.

Drake claimed that he had burned or sunk thirty-seven vessels and captured six others, although the Spaniards officially admitted a loss of only
twenty-four ships in total. Nevertheless the Cádiz division of the Armada
had been almost wiped out, even though there were many other ships
being prepared in Lisbon and a dozen other ports. The financial loss was
over 200,000 ducats, which Philip could ill afford at that time. Indirectly
his loss was much greater, for the bankers lost confidence and raised their
interest rates on their loans to him.

There was still more. Spanish captains had never seen war conducted
in this new fashion and they were thoroughly shaken by the experience.
They did not lose courage, but from that time they steadily lost their
confidence. When they at last set sail for England the next year, it was
hardly in the mood of men about to gain a glorious victory, but almost
that of doomed men in a lost cause.

Drake had learned from the neutral ships and the prisoners he had
taken in Cádiz that a great part of the ships and men, and nearly all the
supplies and armaments for the Armada, had still to come from the
Mediterranean to Lisbon. He decided it was necessary to head for Cape
St. Vincent, that great finger of land jutting out into the Atlantic between
Lisbon and the Straits of Gibraltar, which for the preceding century had
been a recognized station for pirates awaiting their prey. Santa Cruz had a
small squadron of six galleys cruising off this cape, but upon sighting
Drake's formidable fleet they fled for Lisbon at great speed. To remain
cruising there for any length of time Drake knew he must have a port of
refuge nearby to run to in bad weather, and from which he could obtain
fresh water.

On May 4 he landed a thousand men to capture the little town of
Lagos, situated not far from the Cape, but they found it too strongly defended and returned to the fleet having accomplished nothing and having
lost a few men in the process. The next day the fleet moved to Sagres,
which lies on the lee side of the Cape itself, and which has the distinction
of being the site of the school, founded by Prince Henry the Navigator,
where most of the early explorers learned the science of navigation. The
school had been housed in a large castle that now served as one of the
four fortresses guarding the Cape. Drake personally led the attack on this
castle, which looked completely impregnable to attackers with no artillery
of their own. Yet, after a fierce battle, it was captured. The three adjacent

forts also yielded after a struggle, and all were stripped bare of artillery and other things the English fleet could use.

With complete control of the Cape area, Drake left a few ships to cruise there picking up prizes, but moved the rest of his fleet north to Lisbon to seek action with Santa Cruz. The taunts of Drake could not bring the unhappy admiral out to meet him, as his ships were still without guns or men, as most of those at Cádiz had been. Drake was not rash enough to enter the harbor, for Lisbon was even more heavily fortified than Cádiz, and without pilots to guide them through the complicated entrance, Drake's ships would almost certainly have run aground and been an easy target for the heavy guns in the port.

Finding matters so, and with Santa Cruz unable to come out, Drake returned to cruise off Cape St. Vincent until May 23. During all this time his light craft were busy destroying and capturing all shipping, no matter of what nationality, that was carrying supplies for the Armada. Among the many ships captured, there were dozens of small vessels carry- ing barrel staves from various Mediterranean ports. This loss later played an important part in the Spanish disaster in the English Channel. This seasoned wood could not be replaced; the next year the Armada was forced to sail with old and leaking casks for water and wine, and soon after leaving home port ran short of these vital supplies.

A few days after Drake wrote Elizabeth from the Cape that he intended to stay in that area indefinitely, picking up prizes—although he was certain he had accomplished enough to prevent the Armada from sailing that year—he suddenly left for the Azores. He had received news that a great Portuguese carrack returning from the East Indies was due at those is- lands. He realized that he had landed at Sagres and Lagos against the express orders of the queen, and judged that a rich prize would be the best way to soften her anger. Also by that time many of his men were sick with scurvy and other diseases, food was low, and the fleet was ap- proaching the limits of its endurance. He sent some of the sickest men home in several ships, and with the others he sailed westward for the Azores. Immediately a gale scattered them, and several hungry ships turned homeward rather than rejoin him. A few days later a most regret- table incident occurred, which ultimately resulted in all the guilty parties' having their necks stretched on the gallows. The crew of one of the queen's own galleons mutinied because of the shortage of food and of men to man their ship properly. They sent their captain in a small boat to Drake's ship and then deserted, heading for home.

By a remarkable stroke of luck Drake's arrival at the Azores coincided with that of the great carrack, called the *San Felipe,* from the Indian Ocean. She was the most monstrous vessel the English had ever seen, no less than five times larger than any of their own ships. On June 8, near the island of St. Michael, the carrack sailed right into the middle of Drake's fleet, mistaking it for the squadron which should have been there to escort it to Lisbon. After several hours of furious fighting she was taken, but then only because most of her crew and passengers were too sick to fight, having been at sea for over six months by that time. Her cargo alone was worth over 114,000 pounds sterling, more than twice the cost of Drake's entire fleet. With this and the booty picked up in Cádiz and off Cape St. Vincent, the expedition had netted over 140,000 pounds—a great sum indeed, and sure to be welcomed by Elizabeth, or so Drake thought.

Unable to wait for Philip's treasure fleets from the Indies, Drake sailed for England immediately after capturing the carrack and arrived in Plymouth on June 26. Meanwhile, the moment that Philip had heard of Drake's attack on Cádiz, he had sent orders for Santa Cruz to gather all the ships possible and go out to prevent Drake from capturing the West Indian treasure fleets and East Indian carracks. Seizing every ship he could, grabbing men off the streets of Lisbon, including foreigners, snatching nearly all the artillery from the forts of Lisbon, and using even his own money to buy provisions, Santa Cruz managed to outfit a fleet of about forty ships. He set out after Drake, promising a reward out of his own pocket to the man who killed or captured him, but before this fleet ever cleared Lisbon for the Azores, the carrack and its rich cargo had already been captured and Drake's fleet was homeward bound.

Before anything else Philip had to protect his treasure fleets, so that his order to pursue Drake was an urgent and necessary move, although it turned out to be too late. This was the culminating disaster of all those caused by Drake's lightning-fast movements, for in the end it meant that the Armada could not sail that year. Santa Cruz came back to Lisbon in October and found orders from Philip stating that he was to proceed at once with this invasion, but this could not be done as the men were exhausted and the ships required refitting. There was little possibility of supplying these needs before winter set in. Thus the Armada remained in its various ports for the winter, consuming Philip's treasure while doubt gnawed the hearts of the captains.

Drake reached England expecting to pick up reinforcements and new supplies for his squadron and sail again to the Spanish coasts to continue his work of destroying the Armada. To his great amazement, instead of receiving a warm welcome for his outstanding success in preventing the Spaniards from attacking that year, he was very coldly received. Elizabeth and her ministers were embarrassed by his success, because they had still hoped that Philip might be induced to negotiate. Drake had damaged Spain's prestige so much that Spanish pride could not rest satisfied without a fight. Word was sent to Parma that Drake had acted on his own and against the queen's orders, and that she was greatly offended by his piratical actions and meant to punish him thoroughly. She suggested further peace talks and Spain sent representatives to meet with her commissioners in Ostend, a neutral port across the Channel. The talks continued all winter with nothing gained by either side. Elizabeth would have been furious if she had known that Philip was using these talks as a means of deceiving her and that he had no intention of calling off his plans for an invasion. Instead of apologizing for Drake's actions, she should have used them as a threat against Spain.

Philip had intended to proceed with the invasion in the autumn of 1587, but circumstances dictated otherwise. The Duke of Parma was more than eager, as he had already captured the vital seaports needed on the Flemish coast, and the English had no navy except the ships that Drake had led back to England in a very sorry condition. Parma believed that a quick surprise attack would cinch a victory and that since there was no English navy, a small Spanish naval force was all that was necessary to gain and hold command of the Channel. Daily he pressed Philip with dispatches begging that Santa Cruz be sent immediately north to join him in this plan. Philip thought the plan sound and was so anxious to get started that he once wrote to Parma to start without the Armada and undertake the whole operation without any navy. However, the following day he changed his mind and reversed the order, much to everyone's relief.

Philip had told Parma and the Pope early in October that Santa Cruz would reach the Channel before December first, but Santa Cruz had other ideas. Although he still persisted in arguing with Philip that Parma should not be used, and that the army should be carried in the Armada, he knew that he was fighting a losing battle and even told many of his closest aides that the whole scheme was doomed to failure. No doubt these feelings contributed to his reluctance to sail with the Armada immediately as the king wished and had ordered. Common sense was also on Santa Cruz's side, for most seamen knew that it was highly dangerous to sail in the Channel during the winter months.

The situation was complicated still further by Philip's decision not to send any galleys in the Armada, meaning that many galleons would have to be found to replace them. Finally, with sadness, Philip was forced to take fourteen galleons from the West Indian treasure fleets and make them the basis of the Armada's fighting force, along with ten Portuguese galleons that normally were employed in escorting home the richly laden Portuguese carracks. His agents were also still busy buying merchantmen all over Europe, and his shipyards equally busy converting them into warships, although they were much inferior in power to the real galleons.

Some of Elizabeth's advisers recommended that she rely solely on building an army, which would be used in defeating the Spaniards after they had landed on English soil. Luckily the wiser counsel of Sir Walter Raleigh and others prevailed, and the queen was made to understand the importance of a fleet that would encounter the Armada at sea and if possible prevent it from approaching her land at all. All during the year 1587, when Spain's intentions were certainly clear, Elizabeth was being severely criticized for not mobilizing her navy. Sir John Hawkins, her Lord of the Admiralty, was close to hysteria, for none of his demands for funds to meet the cost of readying a fleet was met. Finally, early in December, false news reached London, sending everyone into a panic, that the Armada had already left and was on its way toward England. This finally forced Elizabeth to take action. She mobilized her entire fleet and sent it out cruising in different squadrons. No sooner had all left port than she learned that the news was a false alarm and that the earliest the Armada could possibly sail was early in February.

In the middle of January more information reached her, this time that the Armada's departure had been postponed until March. Although the rest of Europe was certain that war was inevitable, Elizabeth sought desperately to use the delay to strike a bargain with Philip. Dignity forbade her approaching the King of Spain directly, but it could be done through

Parma. She ordered half her fleet laid up and the men discharged, and sent a new group of commissioners to the continent to discuss terms for peace. Philip never slackened his preparations a minute and was more determined than ever to proceed as planned, but the peace talks lasted until the beginning of March, when even Elizabeth realized it was fruitless to continue the farce.

In February Spain suffered a loss that was to have far-reaching consequences for the Armada battle: the death of the Marquis of Santa Cruz, the expedition's leader and Spain's greatest seaman.

After inducing Philip to postpone the Armada's departure until the spring, Santa Cruz had worked feverishly day and night to make the Armada ready, but a visible coolness had grown up between him and the king. Philip, like many small minds raised to high positions, had supreme confidence in his own judgment and refused to entrust his subordinates with authority. He insisted upon regulating everything from the most important plans of the Armada down to the daily habits of every soldier and sailor that would sail on the ships, and the way in which the supplies would be stored. He even intended to direct the actions of the Armada from his own palace hundreds of miles away, using Spain's greatest seaman, Santa Cruz, as little more than an errand boy. Santa Cruz was well aware that after fifty years of service he knew much more about naval affairs than anyone in Spain, especially his king, whose only knowledge of ships came from a few short trips between Spain and the Netherlands. Yet in spite of the difficulties he faced, Santa Cruz carried on faithfully with his work, and it is due to his efforts that the Armada was nearly ready to sail on Februay 9, 1588, when death overtook him. Even though most of Philip's advisers realized that the loss of Santa Cruz meant the loss of almost all hope for a successful expedition, Philip was by no means sorry to be rid of him. He had considered the Admiral far too independent and much too popular to suit his taste.

A year before Santa Cruz died, another death had occurred that also suited Philip's plans. On February 8, 1587, Mary Stuart, Queen of Scots, was executed by Elizabeth's orders. Mary had been held prisoner by her cousin Elizabeth since 1568, when she had been forced to flee Scotland after an uprising, and most men marveled that her life had been spared for so long. In the eyes of all good Catholics, Mary, not the Protestant Elizabeth, was the lawful Queen of England. She had been the inspira-

The Duke of Medina Sidonia

tion for many plots against Elizabeth's life, and it had been assumed that her supporters would join the invasion force in the expectation of placing her on the throne. But Philip did not want Mary, who was in league with France, his greatest rival, on the English throne. With Mary dead, he could make England a Spanish satellite, ruled directly by himself or a member of his family. But both deaths were handicaps to a successful invasion of England: one deprived the Armada expedition of an able leader, and the other deprived it of the main—perhaps the only—source of internal support, so crucial to any foreign invasion.

With the Armada nearly prepared to sail, Philip quickly found a successor to Santa Cruz, a man so ignorant of naval affairs that he had no alternative but to obey Philip's orders blindly down to the smallest detail. This unfortunate man was Alonzo Pérez de Guzmán, Duke of Medina Sidonia. A grandee of the highest rank, enormously rich and fond of riding and hunting, he was a harmless creature, conscious of his defects, without any ambition at all, and happiest when lounging in his garden of orange trees at home. He was nearing the age of forty without having seen active service of any kind. He did hold the title of Captain General of Andalusia, the southern province of Spain, which meant he was in charge of defending those coasts and waters against attack. But his abilities for that task had already been proven sadly deficient only months before, when Drake had attacked Cádiz so successfully.

The duke was dumfounded when he received the news that Philip had given him the great honor of being named Lord High Admiral of Spain and Commander-in-Chief of the Armada. He quickly protested his unfitness, arguing that he was no seaman and knew nothing of fighting on land or water, that even when he ventured out in a rowboat on the river he became violently seasick, and that he knew nothing of politics and cared even less. In short, he wrote to Philip, "I have not one qualification for this post and believe myself the most unfit and unlikely candidate for it."

Philip replied that the duke's reluctance to accept the post could only be due to modesty, but in fact the duke's defects were exactly what Philip wanted in the man for this post. Philip judged that such a man would obey his instructions much more closely than an experienced seamen, would not fight unless necessary, and would not embark on rash adventures. All the king wanted from the duke was to get the Armada to ports where Parma's troops were waiting, then Parma could command even the Armada from that point on. As to seamanship, Philip believed that the duke could rely on the experience of his many aides.

It was characteristic of Spain and Philip that at a time when the whole Armada was ready to sail, when time was of the utmost importance, he wasted six full weeks in correspondence with Medina Sidonia. It was not until March 21 that Philip finally formally appointed the still protesting duke, and still another ten days before the duke received his final instructions.

With doubts and hesitation the duke finally made his way to Lisbon, losing still more valuable time by traveling overland by coach instead of taking the shorter sea route, because the Lord High Admiral of Spain disliked the sea! But once he had arrived he began immediately to inspect the ships under his command, a sight to dismay even the inexperienced duke. Shortly before his death the Marquis of Santa Cruz had reported that the Armada was ready to sail, but during the following two months, when the fleet had been without a commander, everything had turned to chaos.

Many of the men had deserted and in several cases whole ships and their crews had disappeared during the night. Most of the ships stank so badly that the duke had to cover his nose with a perfumed handkerchief. Besides the odors caused by so many men living in confined quarters on vessels that had not been cleaned for ages, there were the smells of salted meat and fish that had decayed, water that had turned putrid, vinegary wine and countless other unidentifiable odors. He found that most of the ships were short of rope, anchors, powder, sails and other equipment, including the most important, artillery. Some of the blame lay with fraudulent contractors who had cheated on the supplies, some with the king for not placing someone in charge until the duke arrived, and lastly a great deal of the blame fell on many Armada officers who were careless or dishonest. The duke discovered that some were even keeping the names of deserters on the rolls and pocketing their pay.

The king had ordered the duke to set sail as soon as he arrived. But

*Armada playing card
showing the Duke of Medina Sidonia
and Admiral Recalde*

Medina Sidonia's first act after inspection was to send a report of the Armada's sorry state and a list of indispensable items without which he would not and could not sail.

The duke was a fussy, anxious man who inquired into everything and meddled with details he could not understand and should have left to his aides. But he soon fancied that though he had never even sailed on a ship before, he already knew more about the sea than officers who had spent their lives commanding ships. When Philip had appointed Don Diego de Valdez as the duke's second-in-command, he had expected the duke to entrust him with most of the important tasks in preparing and commanding the Armada. Valdez, besides being a very famous naval architect and having been at sea for over four decades commanding treasure fleets and making voyages of exploration, was also respected and admired by the other officers. But instead of making good use of his experience and talents, the duke ignored him or gave him unimportant assignments that any of dozens of other junior officers could have handled.

Another major problem in preparing the Armada was that everyone looked upon the venture mainly as a religious crusade against the Protestant heretics instead of as a military operation. Every noble family in Spain had sent one or more of its sons, mainly inexperienced landsmen who knew nothing of the sea or fighting of any kind, to take part in the glorious battle for the Catholic faith. All expected it to be another great victory for Christ like that of Lepanto against the infidel Turks, and no one worried about commonplace things such as obtaining all the necessary supplies or improving the ships' sailing qualities. The king had actually spent almost as much money in donations to churches all over Europe for masses and prayers for the Armada's success as in the actual outfitting of the fleet.

All pains were taken to make the expedition spiritually worthy of its purpose. One of the duke's first orders after taking command was that every single person taking part was to have a voucher from a priest certifying that he had been to confession and had duly commended himself to the Lord. Swearing, gambling, and quarreling were prohibited under pain of severe punishment. The galleons and other ships were named after the apostles and saints into whose charge they were committed, the imperial banners were embroidered with figures of Christ and Our Lady, and on all the mainsails of each ship colorful religious scenes were painted to inspire greater devotion.

If only such energy and imagination had been expended on the more vulgar necessities of the fleet, then the outcome might have been different. Instead, all the rest was mostly left to chance, partly due to a belief that the justness of their cause would insure victory, partly because of Philip's reluctance to part with another ducat, and also because of the impossibility of obtaining all that was needed. The shortage of powder, for example, was without remedy, for after all the powder on hand had been seized from the local forts and from a few merchant ships that entered the harbor, no more was to be had. More serious still, there was no way of replacing the decayed food already stored.

Confused by a flood of conflicting orders and demands from the king, the duke struggled along bravely and actually did extremely well considering that all this was new to him. By the end of April he reported to Philip that he was satisfied with the preparations and would sail shortly. On May 10 he received his final sailing orders from the jubilant but still cautious king. They filled dozens of pages, but the main points were that under no circumstances was the Armada to seek battle; that if they fell in with Drake they were to ignore him even if the coasts of Spain were in danger; and that if a fight was forced on them they must quickly board the enemy because the king knew that the English had better artillery

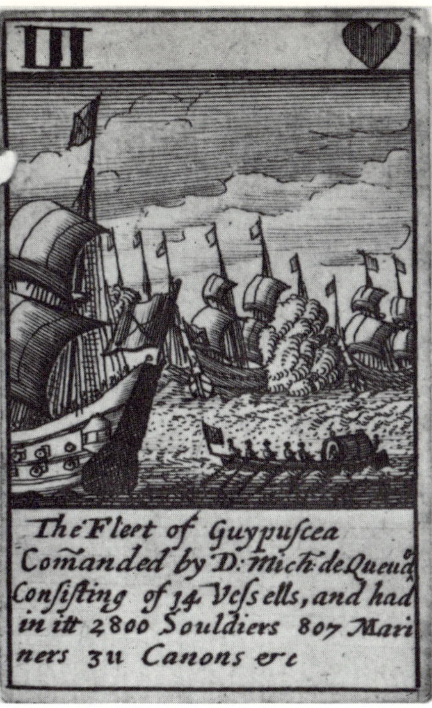

These playing cards were in use in England after the defeat of the Spanish Armada

III
The Fleet of Guypuscea
Comanded by D: Mich: de Queua
Consisting of 14 Vessells, and had
in itt 2800 Souldiers 807 Mari
ners 311 Canons &c

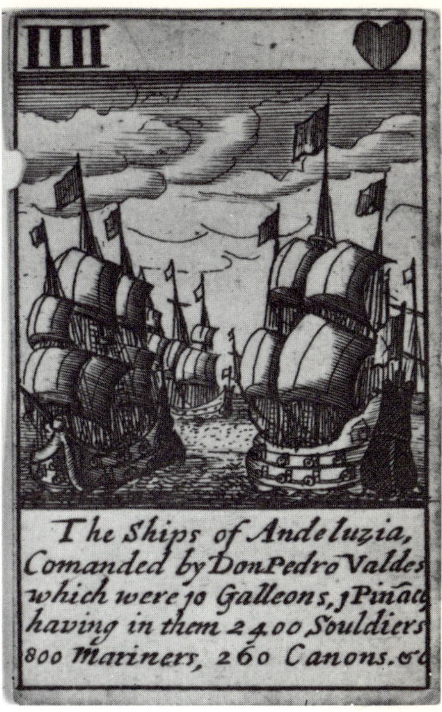

IIII
The Ships of Andeluzia,
Comanded by Don Pedro Valdes
which were 10 Galleons, 1 Pinac
having in them 2400 Souldiers
800 Mariners, 260 Canons &c

and gunners and would try to destroy his ships by superior fire power. Also the Armada was to head straight for the continent to meet Parma, who would then assume command of the entire invasion force.

When finally assembled, the Armada was considerably less imposing than the estimates made by Santa Cruz two years earlier. There were now about 130 vessels of various sizes and types, whose total tonnage—57,868 tons—was actually less than that of a large transatlantic liner like the *Queen Elizabeth*, which is 83,673 tons. Of these vessels seven were over 1000 tons and sixty-seven over 500 tons, but only these could be regarded as fit to take their place in the battle line. So great had been the Spanish needs in the Mediterranean and in the Indies that nearly half of the ships and three fourths of the artillery had been obtained from Protestant contractors in Germany and Denmark, much to the annoyance of the Dutch and English.

The Armada vessels carried over 2500 guns, nearly twice the number that the English fleet had, but all were small—four-, six-, and nine-pounders, more suitable for repelling boarders from the galleys of Barbary pirates than for destroying the large and strongly built English vessels. Worse still, the Spaniards knew little about and cared still less for the science of gunnery. Many still believed that the guns were of little use and that battles would always be fought by grappling and boarding enemy ships, even after Drake's raid in Cádiz had taught the king and many of his top

The Fleete of Castile whereof Diego Flores de Valdes was Generall, consisted of 14 Galleons and 2 Pinnaces, having in it 2485 Soldiers 1719 Mariners, 384 Canons.

The Fleete of Biscay Comanded by Don Ioan Martinez de Recalde which Consisted of 14 Vessells, 2037 Souldiers, 863 Marriners, 200 Canons.

naval officers that the English tactics of fighting with artillery, rather than man-to-man combat on the decks of the ships, were superior. For this reason Philip sent with the Armada a famous Italian who was one of the leading gunnery experts in Europe, yet due to the shortage of powder he could do little to train the ships' gunners before they sailed from Lisbon.

An interesting item on the final list of supplies was the figure of 120,000 cannon balls, yet the Armada carried only 120,000 pounds of powder, when the ratio of powder to shot was four pounds to one, and most of the cannon balls weighed from four to nine pounds each, with some as much as fifty.

Large as the galleons were for their time, they were still very over-crowded. Seamen, soldiers, officers, volunteer gentlemen, surgeons, priests and galley slaves all amounted to around 30,000 men. The soldiers were mainly Italians and Portuguese—less than a quarter were Spaniards. Naturally all the officers, gentlemen, and priests were Spanish. Of the seamen many were just poor farmers and craftsmen who had been impressed into service and really knew nothing about ships.

The Armada was divided into six territorial squadrons, corresponding to Portugal, Castile, Andalusia, Italy, Biscay, and Guipúzcoa, the last two being provinces of the northern coast of Spain bordering on the Bay of Biscay. Most squadron commanders had been wisely chosen for their ability and not for political reasons or family connections, like the Duke

54

of Medina Sidonia. The duke had command of the Portuguese Squadron besides the over-all command of the Armada. Don Diego de Valdez, his second-in-command, or vice-admiral of the whole fleet, was also the commander of the Castilian Squadron, composed entirely of the fourteen galleons and two pinnaces which the king had taken from the West Indian treasure fleet. A cousin of Don Diego, Don Pedro de Valdez, was placed in charge of the Andalusian Squadron, and the Biscayan, Guipúzcoan, and Italian sections were under the equally fine leadership of Martínez de Recalde, Miguel de Oquendo, and Martín de Bertendona, all veterans of Lepanto and countless other battles. Besides these there were several smaller squadrons: the food-and-supply fleet of nearly forty vessels that would not take part in the fighting, four Portuguese galleys that went along for what reason no one ever determined, four newly built Neapolitan galleasses, which were a cross between a galleon and galley with the speed and maneuverability of the galleys and the fire power and strength of the galleons. There was also an assortment of smaller vessels, pinnaces and sloops to be used for reconnaissance and message carrying.

Finally the day that Philip, the Pope, and all Catholic Europe had waited for for so many years arrived. On May 14, after attending a solemn high mass held in the Cathedral of Lisbon followed by a procession in which the Armada was blessed by the Archbishop and special envoys from the Pope, the duke's ship, the *San Martín,* followed by the rest of the

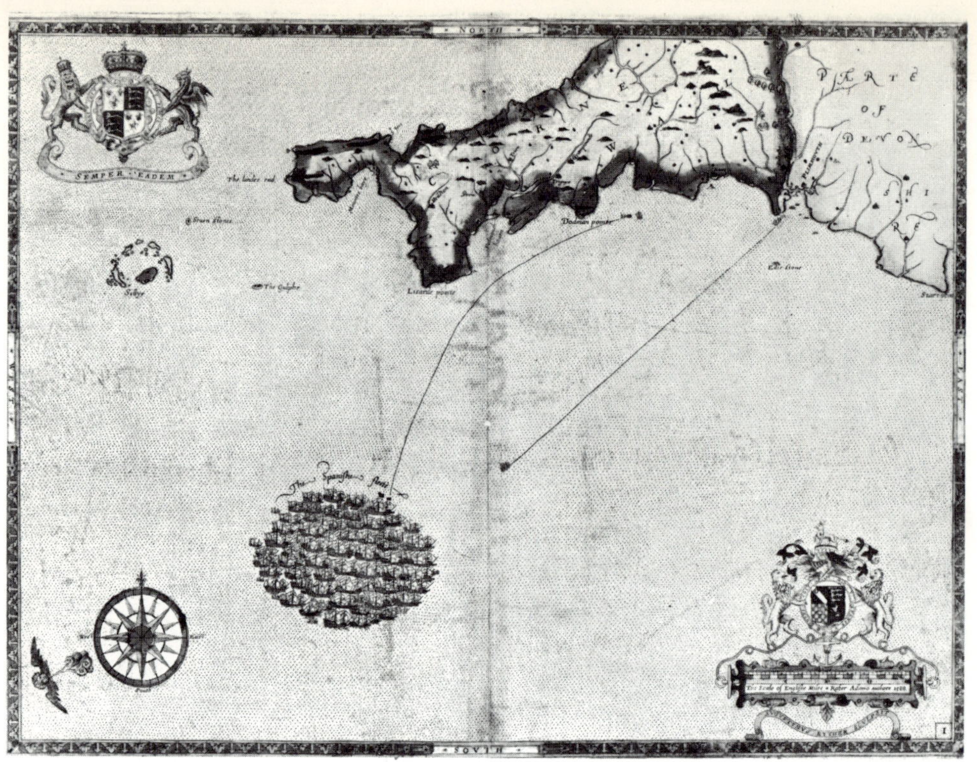

Armada charts

fleet, began moving slowly down the Tagus River with the outgoing tide. Hundreds of musical instruments were playing and the voices of the thousands of men in the fleet could be heard for miles around, plus the great booming of cannon throughout the day, which only wasted precious powder already in short supply.

Bad luck was present from the start. No sooner had the lead vessels begun to cross the dangerous bar at the river's mouth than the wind stopped blowing and the vessels had to drop anchor quickly to keep from being carried onto the rocks and smashed to pieces.

For two full weeks the ships lay rocking on the bar, while the men waited patiently for some wind. During this period, with the fierce southern sun beating down on the men during all the daylight hours—they would have suffocated below decks for lack of ventilation—and the food and water becoming increasingly bad, many men came down with various illnesses, the worst two being dysentery and something called "ship's fever" in those days. Finally on the twenty-eighth the wind came, unfortunately from the north, so that the Armada was blown down off Cape St. Vincent and for two days fought to keep from being blown onto the inhospitable coast of Africa.

As soon as the Armada began to move, its many deficiencies became

56

even more obvious: scarcity of properly trained seamen, too few pilots and none of them acquainted with the English Channel, lack of proper casks and barrels for the liquids, over half of which were lost when the wind started blowing causing the barrels to move about and break open. Friction between the arrogant Castilians and the resentful Portuguese created other problems, and confusion reigned with orders being passed in six different languages and dialects.

The king had expected the Armada to reach the English Channel within ten days after leaving Lisbon. The daily messages bearing the news that the fleet was stranded on the bar of Lisbon nearly drove him mad. Each day as the courier rode up to the gates of the Escorial palace, Philip would be watching from his private quarters and would rush down to snatch the dispatches out of the courier's hand. Everyone, from king to kitchen helper, was certain that each day the good and long-awaited news would arrive, but each day the dispatches brought only word that great numbers of men were succumbing to illness, and many of the ships were developing leaks, among many other problems. On a few ships some men had actually been poisoned by the bad food; on one the poor conditions had caused a mutiny resulting in several hangings.

Their first good fortune arrived on June first when the wind finally

57

shifted to the southwest and at last the Armada began to move northward, but at an unbelievably slow pace. The entire fleet had to move at
the speed of the slowest vessel, and some days it gained barely ten miles.
Yet they were at least making some headway toward their destination, and
the men were a bit happier, knowing that they would soon have the honor
of fighting for the Lord.

The seamen were naturally the busiest, as there is always much to do
on a sailing vessel, even a good ship, let alone old and leaking ones like
most in the Armada. In some, constant manning of the pumps was necessary to keep the water from rising dangerously high in the holds. Most
of the soldiers' time was occupied in simply trying to stay dry and out of
the way of the sailors. Due to the limited space aboard ship there was,
of course, no opportunity for drilling the men.

In those days only a hardy person could endure life aboard a ship, even
on short voyages. There were no quarters for anyone but the highest
officers, and sometimes on the smaller craft not even for them. Everyone
had to sleep wherever he could find a place, and in most cases this meant
out on the open main decks, for there was no space in the holds or on the
lower decks, which were completely filled with supplies and equipment.
Thus when it was rough and seas broke over the gunwales onto the main
decks, and when it rained, the men were completely soaked.

Another hardship resulted from the fact that each man was responsible
for preparing his own food, for the only cooks on board were the personal
servants of the wealthier officers. The only facility for cooking was a stout
iron box called a firebox, generally filled with sand on the bottom so that
an open fire could be made without setting the whole ship on fire. Since
only two or three were carried on each ship, most men never got a hot
meal even when at sea for weeks. The main staple of each man's diet was
a pound and a half of biscuit, a type of dried bread, each day. Even under
ideal conditions it never kept very well and was generally distributed to
the men in a very moldy state and full of weevils. The men would try to
pick them out or just close their eyes and swallow them too. Besides this
each day they would receive either a pound of dried meat or fish and half
a pound of rice or beans, plus an ample amount of vinegar "to make all
the rest eatable." In most cases the men had to eat the meat or fish as it
was—nearly as raw as the day the animal was butchered or taken from the
sea—and the beans and rice went to waste unless they were fortunate
enough to get a turn at the firebox.

Of course the officers, gentlemen volunteers, and clergy ate much better, sometimes even as well as they would ashore. They would bring all sorts of animal and fowl aboard, as well as fresh vegetables and fruit, and usually took for themselves the special delicacies such as chickens, sugar, and eggs carried for the seamen and soldiers who became sick.

Normally there were many diversions to occupy the men's time during the tedious voyages—gambling, mainly, but also plays put on by passengers or seamen, or parties held nearly daily with great quantities of wine to celebrate someone's birthday or saint's day. But on this trip none of these pastimes was permitted, as they were considered unsuitable for a holy crusade, and the men were bored and more quarrelsome than on regular voyages.

The long-hoped-for wind soon turned into an enemy. On the nineteenth, when they were heading on a direct course for the English Channel, a fierce gale struck, scattering the ships about like small corks. Only the day before, the duke had held a council of war of all the admirals of each squadron to decide what should be done about the sick men, the undrinkable water, and the rotten food. The Armada was barely under way and over three quarters of her fighting and working force was out of commission and the supply of food and drink nearly consumed or cast overboard as unfit. They all advised the duke to put into some port for more men, leaving the sick ones to recover ashore, and to obtain more supplies, but, knowing how angry the king would be at such news, he could not make up his mind to do so.

The gale soon decided matters for him. With half of the ships he crawled into the port of Corunna at the northwestern corner of the Spanish peninsula, the weak and hungry crews scarcely able to man the yards. The rest of the ships, scattered by the storm, came in as best they could, some dismasted, some leaking so badly that they had to be run aground on beaches to prevent their sinking. Still others made it into other ports and stayed there until the weather had moderated, but after a week a third of the Armada was still missing, including some of the largest ships.

The first thing the duke did, after ordering a hospital to be set up ashore to care for the thousands of sick men, was to dispatch a pessimistic letter to the king, begging him to cancel the whole expedition until the next year. He described in great detail all the misfortunes that had already befallen the Armada, and suggested that perhaps it was not God's will after all that they invade England. The duke certainly lacked the brave spirit of other Spaniards before him like Cortez, who had conquered all of Mexico with a handful of soldiers, yet in a way he is to be admired for his courage in standing up to the king and expressing his views.

But as soon as Diego de Valdez, the vice-admiral, learned of the duke's letter, he secretly sent one of his own telling the king not to believe all the tales of woe and expressing confidence that their luck would change and that the expedition would be a total success. Philip speedily thanked him for his cheering letter and ordered the duke to stop complaining and get on with the work of his God and his king.

The men obviously shared the duke's feelings about the venture, for many deserted, even though only the sick were permitted ashore and were promptly sent aboard under guard as soon as they recovered, until Valdez persuaded the duke to issue the death penalty and hang any captured deserters.

If it had been up to Valdez, they would have left port the moment the storm abated, even without waiting for the strayed vessels. In some ways he was right, as they still might have been able to surprise the English, and a surprise attack was always considered more important for success than having a stronger force. The Armada had captured every ship as it passed on the high seas, and the king had ordered every foreign ship in Spanish and Portuguese ports to be held there so that they could not carry news of the Armada to England.

It was at this time that the full meaning of Drake's destruction of the barrel staves was realized. This apparently insignificant loss had a disastrous effect. After Drake had burned nearly 90 per cent of the new staves bought for the Armada's use, the king's men had seized or bought all the casks and barrels to be found in the major ports in the peninsula, but as we have seen, most of these were either so old that they broke apart aboard the rolling ships, or the staves were newly cut and the wood still green, so that the contents spoiled. Water and wine were easily obtainable, but almost no containers could be found to store them in, and this deficiency was to be hard felt on most ships in a short time. As for food, that also could be obtained, but it always seemed that the men would eat the fresh supplies as fast as they arrived.

Let us now leave the Spanish Armada and see what the English were up to in the meantime.

Around the beginning of March, when Elizabeth finally realized that

Philip was only using the peace talks to gain time for preparing his Armada, everyone was certain that she would take drastic action against Spain, not only to prevent Philip from executing his plan, but also to retaliate for the humiliation she had suffered in being duped by Philip and the Duke of Parma. Instead, much to everyone's surprise, she did nothing and even forbade her advisers to speak to her about Philip's Armada, or about taking measures to protect her realm. Luckily for England, there were men like Sir Walter Raleigh and Sir John Hawkins, who spent much time, effort, and even their own money in preparing the defenses of England's hundreds of miles of coastline.

Ever since he had returned from his awesome descent on the Spanish peninsula, Sir Francis Drake had never stopped begging the queen to give him the opportunity of attacking Spain again. On May 30 he wrote from Plymouth asking for a fleet of fifty sails to seek battle with the enemy either on their coasts or in their ports, as he had done the autumn before. He stressed that it was no longer a question of just disrupting preparations, but of fighting the concentrated might of Spain that was threatening to descend on England at any moment. The queen never answered his letter, and in mid-April he wrote again in a more urgent tone. Assuming, as was natural, that he would be given command of this fleet, he suggested that someone else be given command of a smaller one that would cruise between the ports held by Parma in Flanders and the English coast facing them, to prevent him from making any surprise attack with his large fleet of troop-carrying barges.

Just as in Spain the most capable naval officers had been bypassed in favor of a titled but inexperienced man to lead the fleet, so too in England. To most people living in those days, as well as those interested in Elizabethan or naval history today, Drake was the only natural choice to command the fleet on which the fate of England depended. However, Elizabeth thought differently. Perhaps she feared that Drake was too adventurous and might dash off after plunder while the dangerous Armada slipped past. The man she selected was one of her distant cousins, Lord Howard of Effingham, as unlikely a candidate for this post as the Duke of Medina Sidonia had been for his. No one had given much thought to the queen's appointment of Lord Howard as First Lord of the Admiralty in 1585, considering it an honorary title that would give him more prestige at the royal court where he spent all his time, but not a duty that

Howard of Effingham

he would actively discharge personally. Actually, until the Armada, Lord Howard had never even stepped on board a ship or taken any part in preparing his navy. All the nautical matters had fallen to Drake and all the administration to Hawkins. Howard's one great advantage over the Duke of Medina Sidonia was that he realized his lack of talent and experience and placed full trust when decisions were needed on men like Drake and Hawkins. This, more than anything else, assured his victory in the end.

62

It came as a great shock when the queen approved of Drake's plan but appointed someone else to execute it. Even worse, she ordered Drake to leave the main fleet in Plymouth and prepare the smaller squadron he had suggested for patrolling the Channel. But Lord Howard had enough sense to see that Drake was indispensable to the success of the plan he had so carefully prepared. Arriving in Plymouth to take command of a fine fleet in peak condition, due solely to Drake's efforts, the first thing Lord Howard did was to arrange with the queen to have another officer, Lord Seymour, command the Channel Squadron, so that Drake could remain as his second-in-command, and to have Sir John Hawkins relieved of his administrative duties in London to join the fleet as third officer.

He soon wrote the queen's secretary that he had formed a war council consisting of Drake, Hawkins, Martin Frobisher and a few other experienced officers and that it was the unanimous opinion of all these gentlemen that Drake's plan of going to Spain to seek battle with the enemy was very sound and should be executed without delay.

Many frustrations still faced the English fleet, due to a combination of changeable weather and a changeable queen. If the Spanish admirals were plagued by incessant orders from their king to set sail without delay even when they were not prepared, the English officers faced the equally exasperating problem of their queen's reluctance to let them sail when the fleet was in complete readiness. First, she ordered Lord Howard to stay in Plymouth because she had received false news that the Armada could not possibly sail for many weeks, and she still hoped somehow that war could be avoided. Then when spies reported that the first news had been false and that the Spanish were ready to sail, and Elizabeth finally gave the signal, they were barely out of Plymouth more than a few turns of the hourglass when a strong southwest gale hit, probably an extension of the wind that had finally enabled the Armada to start heading north.

Forced to re-enter Plymouth until the storm abated, Lord Howard received word from a passing ship that the Armada had finally left Lisbon and he was more anxious than ever to intercept the Spanish before they reached the Channel. Again Elizabeth, fearing that the Armada might slip past her fleet at sea and attack a defenseless England, changed her mind and ordered Howard to remain close to England, covering all possible sea approaches. Replying that he and his officers were sure that the Armada had been forced into some port, since they had left Lisbon more than a month before and had not yet appeared off England's coast, he insisted that they carry through with the original plan of hitting the Spaniards in their own territory. But a new royal dispatch was already on its way from London confining the fleet to port. The queen distrusted the lot of them and was afraid they might try to head for Spanish waters against her orders.

Howard's patience was exhausted and he answered the queen that he and his officers were better able to decide the best course of action, an impudence that surely would have cost him his head if he had not been a member of the family. Worse still, without even waiting for a reply he set sail again on another short, ill-fated cruise. As if in payment for his disobedience, contrary weather forced the fleet back into port again only two days later.

While at sea Howard had received word that several Spanish ships had been sighted off the Scilly Isles, below the southwest tip of England, and he believed that the main body of the Armada might be close behind. Actually these ships were among those that had been separated from the Armada during the gale a few days earlier and they had been driven all the way north to within sight of England. This news was a stroke of luck for Lord Howard and his officers, for it sent Elizabeth into such a panic that she finally entrusted Howard with full responsibility for the fleet's movements rather than risk the delays in transmitting advice and orders back and forth between Plymouth and London.

After a few days had passed and there was no sign of the Armada or news of other Spanish ships, Howard and Drake decided that the ships reported earlier had been a false alarm. They amassed a sufficient store of victuals and beer—English sailors drank beer with all their meals instead of wine like the Spaniards—and for the third time they left Plymouth, on June 24, with the plan of heading directly for Spain. Again the wind turned foul and for two weeks the fleet could barely hold its own; the ships were strung out across the Channel for miles, doing their best to keep afloat and keep from being blown into the North Sea. By the time the wind turned fair again, Howard had decided it would be best to wait in those waters for the Armada, since they really had no information on its position. Only Drake's threats to go on his own, hinting that many of the other ships would probably follow him, induced Howard to continue on toward Spain.

The Spanish Armada off Lizard Point

The southerly course was taken on July 7, but when the English fleet was still short of the Spanish coast, once again a southwesterly gale struck them and forced them to turn about and run with it. For the third and last time in these heartbreaking circumstances, they entered Plymouth on July 12, very short of victuals and with many men sick from the same illnesses that plagued the Armada's crews. At about that time news also arrived of the Armada's bad fortune, but it was misleading, for it indicated that the Armada had been canceled for that year. Fortunately for England, however, Howard, Drake and the others decided that this was a unique opportunity for another venture. The Spanish West Indian treasure fleets and the Portuguese East Indian carracks would soon be approaching the Spanish peninsula unescorted, for the entire Armada was disabled and the English could capture them without a struggle. It was with this plan in mind that the English were occupied with revictualing and repairing their vessels when, on July 29, word came that the whole Spanish fleet had been sighted near the Lizard, the southwest point of England, and in a few hours would be off Plymouth.

When Philip had received that first very discouraging letter from the Duke of Medina Sidonia, after the Armada had been forced into Corunna,

65

he rushed there one of his closest advisers, Don Jorge Manrique, to insure that the Armada sailed again promptly. Upon arriving and meeting the duke for the first time, Manrique wrote to the king that as long as the duke remained in command of the Armada, there was no chance of success. He begged the king to replace the Duke with Valdez or someone else with more experience and enthusiasm and assured Philip that all the senior officers desired this change. Martínez de Recalde, commander of the Biscayan Squadron, also wrote to the king advising a change in plans. The season was getting late, he explained, and if the Armada were struck by bad weather before England had been completely conquered, they would have no port of refuge. He felt that the sensible thing would be to secure an English port such as Dartmouth or Plymouth even before joining with Parma's army. But Parma had already been waiting in several ports in Flanders for nearly a year, ready to embark his troops the moment the Armada appeared, and for two months he had been blockaded by a strong Anglo-Dutch squadron, unable even to bring in supplies for his army. So for that reason Recalde's plan was completely unacceptable.

Three weeks were to pass before every ship from the Armada reached Corunna to join the main force. Fresh meat was obtained, new biscuit baked, and the crews and soldiers quickly regained their health on a diet of fresh food and good water—only a handful actually died from the various epidemics. More men were found to fill the place of the deserters and everyone seemed to acquire a new zeal to get under way once again, with the exception of the duke. But even he finally came around when he received a vigorous letter from the king on July 15 commanding him to set sail within a week or face severe punishment from his already too patient king. This time the duke knew that his life was at stake and began immediately to embark all the men and set the victualers to work around the clock to complete the provisioning.

At sunrise on the twenty-second of July the weather was sparkling and most of the old salts predicted good weather for the remaining two months of the summer, at the end of which time they expected the whole conquest of England to be over and the Armada to be snug in some Spanish port before the harsh winter weather set in. The Armada, a good deal happier than when it had arrived in Corunna, made its second start. There were a few minor changes in composition, but it still consisted of 130 vessels and around 30,000 men. This time at least their victuals were in a much

*Don Juan Martínez
de Recalde*

better state, although unfortunately the same could not be said for their water and wine rations, still carried in the same rotten barrels. Also several pilots had been found who knew the English Channel very well, and the duke was even able to have them draft a set of proper sailing directions for these unfamiliar northern areas where very few Spanish vessels had ever ventured. Each ship in the Armada received one, in case any should be parted from the main body of the fleet by bad weather.

By July 23 the last of the vessels of the Armada, which at that time was stretched out for ten miles, had passed the last cape in Spain. The weather, as if to make up for past persecution, blew fair and steady from the south. For the next few days the men grew more tense as they rapidly approached the coast of England. Good luck held for a while, however, and at sundown on the evening of the twenty-fifth the duke found himself with all his flock about him at the mouth of the English Channel. Much to everyone's surprise not an English vessel or one from any other nation that could have rushed ahead to warn the English was in sight. The men witnessed one of the most brilliantly colored sunsets any of them had ever seen and most took it as a sign of good weather ahead and of sure victory over the enemy. However, many of the pilots and old sailors proclaimed that it was a sure sign that bad weather was near.

The following morning broke calm and cloudy, then light northerly winds came which halted their progress, soon followed by heavy showers that helped conceal the mass of ships but also placed them in danger of collision with one another. By this time, since no vessels of any nationality had been sighted, the duke believed that either England had no naval force at all, or was too intimidated to face his formidable force.

The night passed without event except a minor fire on one of the smaller vessels. Although it was quickly extinguished, the duke feared it might have been seen at a great distance, revealing the Armada's presence. As day broke the northerly breeze swung around to the west, which was to their advantage, but a few hours later it increased in force and soon was blowing a full gale. The waves became so high that they broke clear over the stern castles of the galleons, in some cases sweeping men out to sea. The Armada had to heave to and ride it out. One of the galleys received such serious damage that it had to head back for Corunna, but was lost on the way and disappeared without trace. The skeptics who had predicted this event were themselves so frightened they had no chance to say "I told you so." Around noon on the twenty-eighth the storm abated but there was still a very heavy swell running, making the ships roll over as much as fifty degrees on each side and causing the loss of many artillery pieces that in some cases carried parts of the wooden hulls with them. The ships were all unmanageable, and it was discovered that forty of the vessels were missing. The remaining three galleys had had to make for the coast of France or risk being swamped, for they had not been designed to withstand such seas. The large galleon *Santa Ana*, flagship of the Biscayan Squadron, had disappeared completely and was reported to have sunk. Actually it had become separated from the Armada and had developed very serious leaks, so that it also had had to head for the French coast.

Much to the duke's relief, the rest of the missing ships were found to be only a few miles ahead. The Armada was complete again except for the galleys, which were really of little use in these waters, and the *Santa Ana*. With the sky clearing from the southwest, the fleet continued on its way up the Channel.

They still had not seen anything—not even a small fishing boat—but as they were already on the enemy's coast, they arranged themselves into fighting formation and battle stations were maintained on all vessels, with artillery pieces run out and lighted matches ready for igniting the powder. They were formed into three divisions: the duke took up the center with the main body of fighting vessels, Alonzo de Leyva had the honor of leading the vanguard, and the rear guard was under the command of Martínez de Recalde, for fortunately he had transferred from his leaking flagship *Santa Ana* to his vice-admiral's ship before the gale had begun. The whole formation resembled a crescent, like a new moon, with de Leyva and Recalde at the two tips.

Maintaining their positions in this formation, they sailed slowly on through the rest of the day, still out of sight of land but knowing by certain observations and by making soundings that they were approaching the coast. Finally, around four that afternoon, the gray ridge of the Lizard rose above the sea through the haze, three leagues off. Now they were actually in sight of the cave of the dragon they had come to slay. The duke ran up a special flag of his own that had been embroidered for the occasion—Christ on the Cross with Our Lady kneeling below in prayer. As it unfurled in the breeze, each ship fired a broadside which could be heard even ashore by the fearful inhabitants of that coast, and the ships' companies gathered on the main decks and prayed in thanks for arriving that far safely and to ask God for a victory.

That evening the duke wrote his last letter to the king: "So far," he said, "the enemy has not shown himself, and I am now moving forward in the dark. Before me lie only the silent sea and the long Cornish coast, marked at intervals by columns of smoke which I suppose are alarm signals. No word has come from Parma. I have a premonition of great danger, and I fear I must disregard your explicit orders. Until I hear from Parma I will move no farther up the Channel than the Isle of Wight, anchoring there as long as is necessary." That night the duke gave orders to reduce sail and the Armada barely moved at all. Valdez and the other officers should have arrested the duke and taken over command. Unfortunately for them, and fortunately for the English, they did not.

The entire next day, as the Armada continued to creep along slowly and cautiously, the duke waited anxiously for the return of any of the many small reconnaissance boats he had sent out the evening before. Those that returned reported much activity on the shore—the English were preparing defenses to repel any invasion—but they had not seen one sail. It was not until shortly after midnight that one of the fast pinnaces arrived with four fishermen they had captured from a Falmouth smack. Without even having to resort to torture, the Spaniards learned from the frightened prisoners that Drake and Lord Howard had already come out with most of their fleet and were lying in wait for the Armada in Plymouth Sound.

Early on the morning of the twenty-ninth the pinnace *Golden Hind*, one of Drake's patrol vessels, had come flying into Plymouth Harbor under full sail, running so fast that it never even took time to salute the fort and was nearly blown out of the water before the officer in charge recognized the vessel. The commander, a Captain Fleming, quickly sprinted ashore in search of Drake, whom he found enjoying a leisurely game of bowls on Plymouth Hoe with several other officers. Almost out of breath, the captain burst out the news that the Armada was off the Lizard and proceeding slowly in their direction before a southwest wind. But Drake amazed everyone by ordering his companions to continue, saying, "We have enough time to finish this game and then attend to our adversary."

It seemed as if the Spaniards would now catch the English in the very same predicament they had been in in the past. With the English ships cooped up in a narrow harbor and with the breeze blowing toward land, the Spaniards could loose a few fireships at the mouth of the harbor and destroy the whole fleet. But Drake was neither stupid nor irrational. He realized that the tide was against him and that the fleet could not leave until the next change of tide, that evening, so instead of flying into a panic that would affect the whole fleet, he took the only course—to remain calm and finish his game of bowls. He and Howard did order the ships quickly

The imperturbable Sir Francis Drake continues his game of bowls

manned and prepared for battle, but they could do nothing of real importance until the tide should change and permit them to leave. A council of war was called that afternoon in which it was decided that they would leave the harbor that night and try to get to windward of the Armada. Then they could wage war by standing off and relying on their superior gun power, rather than risk being boarded by the Spaniards' more numerous forces.

Little time was lost in executing this maneuver. As soon as the tide started flowing outward all ships were darkened, crews were placed at their battle stations, and ships were warped out of the harbor against the incoming breeze. By sunup the best part of the fleet was beating to windward; by noon the entire fleet of fifty-four ships had cleared Plymouth Sound and the lookouts in the crow's nests sighted the mast tops of the Armada. The wind died out and the fog came rolling in, forcing them to take in all sail and wait better conditions. Meanwhile many privately owned vessels manned by patriotic civilians began to join the fleet from various ports.

As the moon rose, just about the time that the Spanish pinnace reached the duke's flagship, the wind began to reappear, light but enough to enable the English to put on sail again and try to get to the windward of the Armada. Some of the English ships sailed so close across the bows of the Spanish ships that voices could be heard, but the night was still cloudy and they passed unseen. In fact the only information the Spanish had on their movements was from the captured fishermen.

Meanwhile the duke had made another of his many serious blunders. By ordering the Armada to anchor for the night, he enabled the enemy to gain the windward position, the most advantageous in a sea battle and one they held nearly continuously for the next ten days. If he had kept moving he not only could have prevented this but also would probably have sailed right into the middle of the English fleet, boarding and cap-

Tapestry of the Spanish Armada

turing them while they were unable to make use of their long-distance cannon. His most serious error had been to reduce speed the moment the Armada sighted the Lizard, giving the English more time to prepare for battle. Otherwise the Armada could have reached Plymouth and destroyed the English fleet right in the harbor.

The duke met stiff opposition from the other admirals about anchoring for the night. Most were not afraid that the English would swoop down on the stationary ships in the dark but felt that they were in a very dangerous position if an onshore breeze should start. Recalde once again urged the capture of an English port to be used as a haven for the Armada, suggesting Plymouth as the best choice, since the English had left it. Most of the other admirals were against this idea, however, for then they would only be exchanging places with the English fleet—putting themselves in the uncomfortable position of being crowded into a small harbor where they would be vulnerable to attack from fireships. Nothing was really decided except that at first light they would weigh anchor and continue the voyage, fighting the English only if attacked, as the king had ordered. By the time the council of war was over and the admirals had started back for their respective flagships, lookouts were straining their eyes for sight of the English fleet.

IV

S THE HAZE BEGAN TO CLEAR and the sun rose, the Spanish lookouts searched the horizon between them and the coast and to
the northeast where the English fleet had last been reported. To
their great surprise, only eleven English ships were in front of them, but
forty others were to their rear. The Duke of Medina Sidonia was dumfounded when he received this report, claiming that the Devil himself must
have helped the English heretics execute such a brilliant feat of seamanship
and gain the windward position. The eleven ships ahead, led by Howard,
swiftly sailed past the Armada and out of the range of cannon fire to join
the other forty led by Drake, even before the Spaniards could pull up their
anchors and put on sail.

Upon joining the main body of the English fleet, Howard assumed
command and ordered the ships to form in a single file, to maintain their
windward position at all costs, and to destroy the Armada by long-range
cannon fire. While watching the English regroup and form into their battle line, the Duke of Medina Sidonia was heard to remark, "Surely these
ill-bred heretics are not stupid enough to attack my powerful Armada
when our ships outnumber them nearly three to one."

He went on to criticize the appearance of their ships, claiming that
they were all very badly designed and were totally unfit for use in sea
battles. They were very unlike the high-towered bulky Spanish galleons:
Hawkins had reduced the huge castles at stern and prow on all English
warships, and increased the length of their hull while narrowing their
beam. The end result was that the slowest of the English ships could still

sail twice as fast as the fastest Spanish ship; they could all sail much closer to the wind, were ten times more seaworthy in good or bad weather and, having lower silhouettes, were harder to hit with cannon fire. Of course the duke did not realize at the beginning what all these improvements meant, but he was to learn all too quickly.

According to Spanish ideas on naval tactics, the English fleet, even though vastly outnumbered, should have charged into the larger force and boarded the ships of the rear guard to capture or destroy them quickly before the others could come to their rescue. As long as the wind kept in the same position, the English could then advance, attacking the rest of the ships at will, until they had won the battle. Even though the risk was great, the Spaniards were certain that the English would follow this plan. But this assumption was as wrong as the duke's criticism of English naval design.

What a surprise he must have had when the whole English fleet, with Drake in the lead, decreased the distance between both fleets and began to pass close-hauled in line behind the Armada, sweeping the ships of their rear guard with devastating fire. Broadside after broadside crashed into the ships of Recalde's squadron, the English firing five rounds to each of those fired by the confused and badly trained Spaniards, and all the English balls were more accurately aimed and much larger in caliber. In order to return the cannon fire, Recalde had to halt his ships and turn them broadside to the passing English battle line. The duke should have stopped the whole Armada to prevent his rear guard from being cut off by the enemy, but he permitted the rest of his fleet to continue on its easterly course, leaving Recalde behind to face the enemy alone. This blunder was shortly followed by another. Lookouts reported that a dozen or more English ships were trying to sneak out of Plymouth Sound to join the English fleet, stationed between the coast and the Armada. He turned the main body of the fleet toward land and began to give chase, but of course every one of the faster English vessels was able to escape.

By this time Recalde's squadron had for hours been standing alone against the whole naval might of England. When the duke learned of their serious plight he ordered the whole Armada to rush to their rescue. The first to reach them were naturally the four galleasses and some smaller pinnaces able to use their oar power against the wind. Under the rain of hundreds of shot fired from the enemy, these ships quickly passed cables

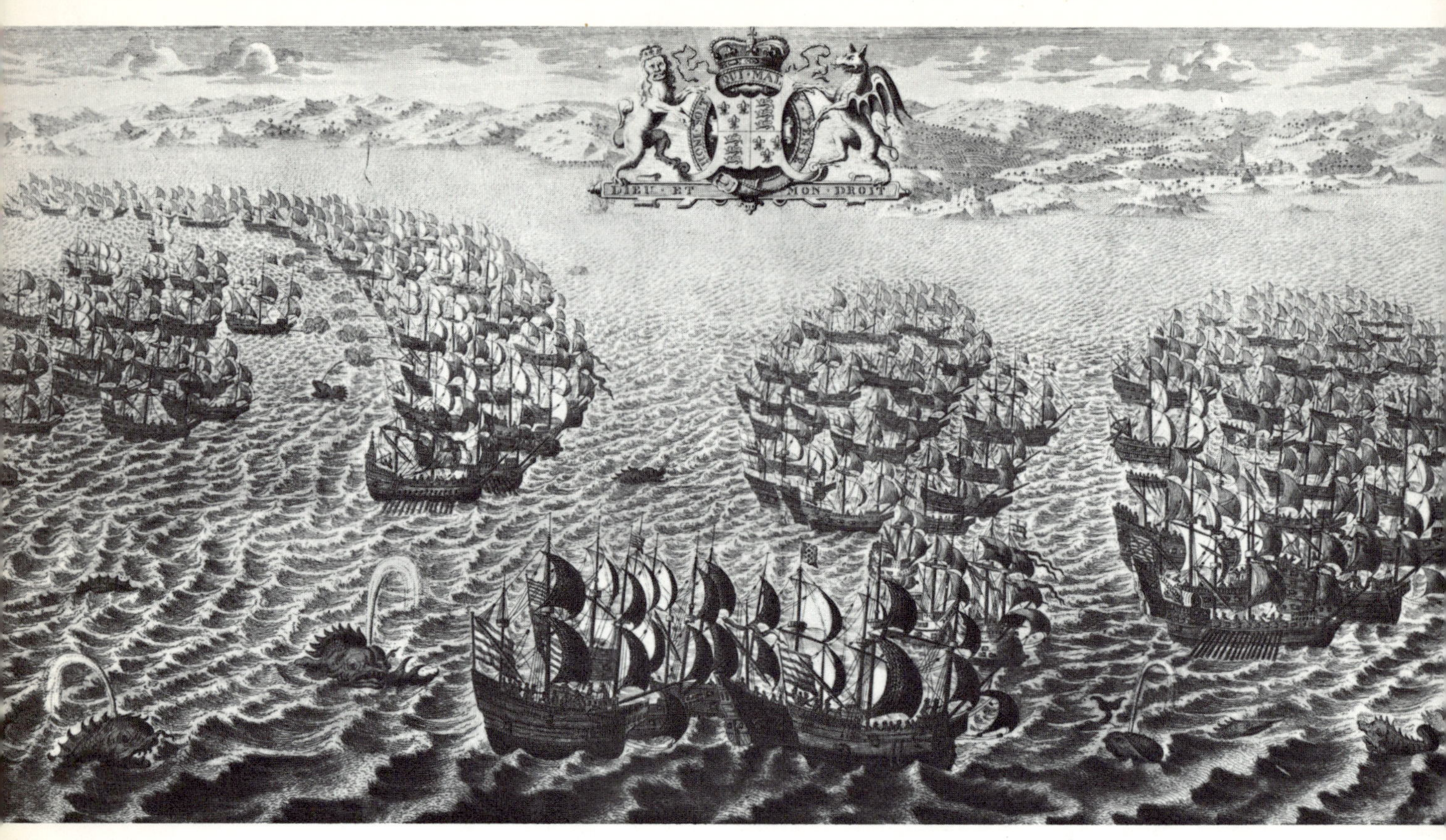

The first engagement: the first break of the crescent

to the more seriously damaged ships and began to tow them away from the inferno, themselves receiving a great deal of damage in the rescue operation.

When they finally rejoined the rest of the Armada, Drake and Howard were close behind, but, unwilling to risk a general engagement, they simply moved their battle line farther away and resumed fire with their long-range guns for the rest of the day. The Spanish cannon had a much shorter range and so were unable to do much damage in return.

The battle, if such it could be called when the Armada had been nothing but a helpless target, lasted until four in the afternoon. Although no Spanish ships had been sunk or captured, many had lost masts and rigging, and some had suffered holes below the waterline. All this could be repaired but hundreds of men on the crowded decks had been killed or wounded from shot and flying splinters. The duke and many of his officers were forced to admit that they had underestimated English power and skill.

76

The Armada's advance up the Channel had not been halted, but it was perfectly obvious to the Spaniards that, unless there was a change of wind, the English could continue to harass them, weakening the Armada in such a way that by the time it reached the meeting point with Parma, it would be of no value in protecting the invasion forces.

The day's misfortunes were not yet over. As the sun set, the Armada was proceeding up the Channel with the enemy fleet close behind. Repairs were being made on all the ships of Recalde's squadron at a furious pace, and many divers and carpenters had been sent aboard his flagship, which was in danger of sinking. Suddenly it fell behind. Pedro de Valdez decided to drop back and see what help he could lend Recalde, his closest friend. Swinging his ship about, he collided with another galleon and broke his bowsprit and foretopmast, which made his vessel unmanageable. On board this galleon, one of the best in the whole Armada, were over 500 men, a large sum of money and, among other treasures, a chest of jewel-studded swords sent by King Philip to English Catholic nobles in gratitude for their past efforts in the Catholic cause.

Don Pedro de Valdez

Don Miguel de Oquendo

As it was almost dark already and the weather was becoming fouler each minute, the duke ordered the Armada to continue on its way, leaving Don Pedro and his ship to their own fate. Two of the squadron commanders jumped into longboats to complain to the duke of this unjust order, but their protests went unheeded, as he refused to risk the whole Armada for the sake of one ship. Still it is a mystery why he did not send at least two of the galleasses to take the damaged ship in tow as had been done with Recalde's galleon. Although the majority of the crew was finally rescued by several small boats, Valdez and about fifty men remained on board along with the treasure, expecting to be attacked at any moment.

Shortly afterward disaster struck again. Around midnight all the leaders were gathered in a council of war on the duke's galleon when a great explosion was heard, at first believed to be a night attack from the English. A serious quarrel had broken out between the sailors and the soldiers on Oquendo's flagship while he and his senior officers were away. Whether by accident or deliberately, someone in the fight had dropped a torch near the powder magazine, which quickly exploded, destroying the whole internal structure of the galleon as well as all her masts and rigging, leaving nothing but an outer shell and most of that burning. Over 200 men were killed and not one escaped injuries.

78

Luckily no other ships were close enough when the accident occurred to be hit by burning timbers that flew in all directions. The nearest vessels quickly sent boats to pick up the over 300 injured survivors that had been blown into the water. Others were sent on board to extinguish the fire and try to save the ship from sinking, but by the following morning it was so low in the water it could not even be towed and had to be abandoned.

Even before the Armada had left Lisbon it had been constantly pursued by bad luck. The two calamities of that day had cost them two fine galleons and a heavy loss of men, and this, following the unexpected failure against the enemy, chilled the spirits of the whole Armada. Yet what upset the officers and men more than anything else was the duke's desertion of Don Pedro de Valdez and his ship. Not only was this a blow to national pride and prestige, it was also a loss of one of the greatest seamen in the whole fleet and many brave men.

When the Spaniards saw the next morning that the English fleet was still behind them but widely scattered in no apparent formation and too distant to use their cannon, they wondered what new trick the English devils were up to. They could not know that, far from a new tactic, this was the result of a comical but almost tragic mishap.

Lord Howard had also called a council of war on board his flagship the preceding night in which all his officers had decided they would keep their windward position, close on the heels of the Armada and ready to act if the Spaniards should try to seize the Isle of Wight, the last possible port of refuge before crossing to the continent. Drake had been given the lead position and had hung a bright lantern on the stern of his ship as a marker for the rest of the English fleet to follow. At first all went well, until one of Drake's lookouts reported ships to landward moving in the opposite direction. Always the daring adventurer, Drake decided to pursue what he thought were Spanish ships trying to sneak past to attack the English from the rear. He could have dispatched a small boat to order another ship to investigate, but instead he extinguished the stern lantern and set off on his own, leaving the whole English fleet in confusion with no signal to follow.

At first light the next morning, Lord Howard found his own ship hard against the rear guard of the Armada with only a few other English ships in sight. Before the Spaniards could take advantage of Howard's dangerous position, he and the handful of other English ships dropped back and

The Ark Royal

went in search of the rest of the fleet. Gradually they were all found and
began to regroup again, Drake's being the last to rejoin the rest, in the
middle of the afternoon. Howard was naturally very angry and many
thought he would order Drake sent ashore in chains. He summoned him
aboard his flagship, the *Ark Royal*, and demanded an immediate explana-
tion.

Drake found it all very amusing and told the story with his usual calm.
The ships he had chased turned out to be peaceful German merchantmen
and were left to continue on their course. By then it was daylight and
while returning to the fleet Drake claimed he accidentally sighted the
damaged Spanish galleon of Don Pedro de Valdez, which was then gal-
lantly defending itself against a smaller English ship, which needed a
helping hand. Without even firing a shot he sent word to Valdez advising
him to surrender, which the Spaniard promptly did, not considering it a
disgrace to yield to such a renowned captor as Drake. Don Pedro was
brought aboard to drink a toast with Drake, then sent back to the galleon,
which was taken into Dartmouth by men off Drake's ship. Besides the

80

treasure aboard this prize, there was found a precious store of powder, of which the English were already in sore need. Once ashore, Don Pedro and his surviving crew were given good treatment and were later ransomed. They were at least spared the further pain of serving under the incapable leadership of the Duke of Medina Sidonia.

Drake had many enemies who were jealous of his fame and popularity, some of them right in the English fleet. When Howard did nothing to punish Drake for his rash act, one of the senior officers wrote the queen spreading the false rumor that Drake had deserted the fleet and left it in deadly peril only because he wanted to capture a rich Spanish prize. This was a very unjust accusation. No one in the English fleet had witnessed the collision, and in the darkness the whole fleet had sailed right past the galleon without seeing it, except for the last vessel, which had come to investigate. Although Drake was definitely in the wrong for deserting his post as guide for the whole fleet, he was innocent of this other charge.

The following night about an hour after midnight, as both fleets were becalmed about a league apart without a breath of wind to ruffle the smooth sea, three of the Spanish admirals—de Leyva, Recalde, and Oquendo—came on board the *San Martín*, woke the duke out of one of his rare moments of peaceful sleep and, burning with indignation, demanded that he take action to restore the honor of Spain, which they declared had been lost during the last two days. Taking him out on the quarterdeck,

Capture of the Valdez galleon

Drake receiving the surrender of Valdez

they showed the duke by the light of the moon how the English ships had drifted apart during the calm and, without wind, were now deprived of their advantage of speed and maneuverability. They had already worked out a plan which they unfolded for the sleepy duke. The four galleasses would be sent out and, making use of their oar power in the calm, could destroy single English vessels by attacking each one from all four quarters at once, hoping to overpower many before the night was over.

They went on to explain that if the wind rose around sunrise from the east as expected, then the whole Armada would have the windward position and could swoop down on the English. The success of the plan depended on speed and surprise, but the duke wasted several hours studying the details before he finally gave his approval. By the time the four galleasses were on their way, bearing down on several isolated English ships, the sun was already rising. The wind did start up from the east as predicted, giving the Spaniards the windward position for the first and only time during the many days of battle, but they were too slow to take advantage of it, and their commander once again proved himself an incompetent naval officer.

82

The galleasses had to call off the attack as the wind freshened, as they were unable to withstand the rough weather. The rest of the Armada bore down with all sails set on the surprised English fleet, and Lord Howard's *Ark Royal,* which was very close at hand, had to come about and stand off to sea. In doing so, it was forced to cut right through the middle of the advancing Armada. Other ships of the English fleet were in similar circumstances and had to follow the flagship with the result that both fleets became intermixed. At one time there were over a dozen large Spanish galleons around the *Ark Royal,* but several other English vessels came to her rescue and together they managed to free themselves from the mass of surrounding Armada ships.

Once again the duke had made a serious mistake. Helped by the sudden appearance of the east wind, the Spanish had been able to cut the English fleet in two, leaving over half trapped between the shore and the Armada, unable to follow Howard and the few others who had escaped to open water. But instead of ordering his ships to head toward the coast and attack those inshore vessels, which were also faced with the danger of shoal water to their east and west, the duke foolishly ordered the Armada to chase after Howard and his companions. He should have realized by then that with the exception of the four galleasses, which were useless in the rough sea, none of his ships could possibly sail as fast as the English. Thus while the Armada was engaged in a fruitless pursuit of faster vessels that had the open ocean before them, all the English ships that had been trapped on the coast, and which everyone from Lord Howard to the spectators on the shore expected to be easy prey for the Spaniards, were able to escape easily and rejoin the other half of the fleet.

Then around noon, with most of the Armada scattered over a wide area after its frustrating chase, the wind swung almost completely around to the southwest, returning the windward position to the English. Suddenly, out of the dense smoke produced that morning during the cannonades, the Spanish saw at least fifty warships bearing down on them, led by Drake and Frobisher. The duke's galleon, easily recognized by its many flags and banners, was the main target of the attack. Besides losing nearly all of her rigging, she received over fifty holes through her double-planked hull, and over half of her crew were killed or wounded. At times the English ships, especially Drake's, came within 100 yards of the *San Martín* and let loose tremendous broadsides. Other times enemy broadsides would strike her from both sides at once, and it seemed as if she would be battered to pieces. Only about a dozen other Spanish ships close to the *San Martín* were actually in the battle too. The enemy ships were so closely packed around these that the rest of the Armada vessels were unable to come to their aid.

Toward sunset the wind began to fall, forcing the English fleet to bear away and stop the action, rather than take a chance of being caught in another calm close to the Armada where they would be the target of another and possibly more successful attack from the Spanish galleasses.

The Duke of Medina Sidonia had uneasily observed from his badly shattered quarterdeck that his pursuers, steadily reinforced by private vessels, were growing more numerous, and although he had lost only two vessels so far, his casualties were very high and powder and shot were rapidly running out. He had already written to King Philip of his intention of stopping at the Isle of Wight, and that evening he called another council of war in which all the leaders agreed with this plan. They would steer a course directly for the island and land 10,000 soldiers to occupy it. They also decided to leave a permanent garrison after the Armada had left to join Parma, because it could serve as a base for a smaller invasion to be launched at the same time the main army landed near Dover.

At the end of the day's battle the English fleet was nearly out of powder, for the queen had been able to provide only two days' supply at the start. All the following day dozens of small boats were plying to and from the fleet bringing badly needed ammunition and food and carrying the wounded back to shore. Also by that time all England had the news of the Armada's arrival, and many privateering and merchant vessels had been rushing to join Lord Howard. By noon both fleets were nearly equal in size.

Ashore thousands of people were congregated on the beaches, many having traveled long distances to witness this great spectacle. That day they were very disappointed, for it was flat calm and neither fleet was able to move.

That night final plans for the invasion of the Isle of Wight were discussed on board the duke's flagship. It was decided that the Armada would anchor in the Solent, the body of water between the island and the English mainland, and remain there until more munitions and men were sent by Parma. The duke told his officers that he was positive they would be successful because the following day was the feast of Saint Dominic, the patron saint of his illustrious family.

Thursday morning, August 4, broke with a light breeze from the west. The Armada was by then off the southwest point of the Isle of Wight, having passed the western entrance to the Solent with the plan of entering from the eastern side, a safer route. The English were fully aware of the Spanish plan to capture the island, as reports had reached Lord Howard from the commander of the island's fort that several small Spanish craft had been seen taking soundings in the Solent and off several beaches where no doubt the troops would disembark. The night before, the landward half of the English fleet had moved up closer to the Armada, placing themselves in a position to attack the landing force, and the other half had come so close to the Armada's rear guard that insults shouted back and forth between the two forces were heard all night long.

Shortly after sunrise, when all the Armada ships were busily preparing their landing forces, the Duke of Medina Sidonia suddenly decided to postpone the landing. Many of his associates claimed that he had surely lost his head. He had seen that half of the English fleet was once again between the shore and the Armada, giving him the same opportunity to drive them against the coast that he had missed two days before. He ordered the Armada to attack immediately, and the "no quarter" flag was hoisted on the *San Martín*, meaning that any prisoners taken would be

Action off the Isle of Wight

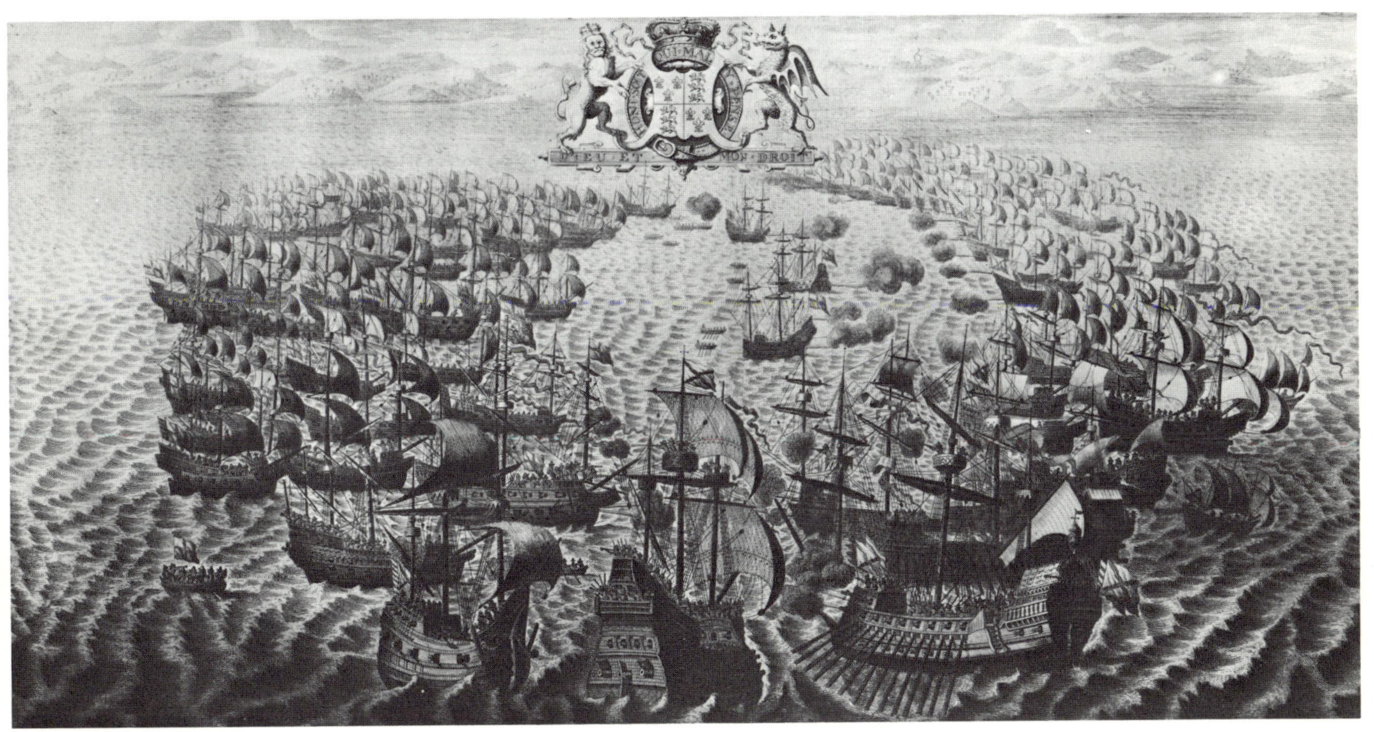

Lord Howard on the Ark Royal, *engaging the ship of Don Alonzo de Leyva*

put to the sword. The duke really believed that the Spanish ships would finally have the chance to close in on the English and permit his thousands of frustrated soldiers to board their ships and overwhelm them with superior numbers.

But that chance never came. Even before half the Armada had come about to head toward the landward part of the English fleet, Howard realized what their plan was and ordered the rest of his ships, which were right on the heels of the Spaniards, to attack immediately. The duke had failed to make any plans for repelling this force, and many of his officers later commented that he must have thought that Howard and the rest of the English would simply watch the Armada destroy half of their fleet without doing anything.

Howard's *Ark Royal* led the attack, charging right into the center of the Armada, but this ship had outsailed her consorts and quickly found herself alone surrounded by Spanish galleons. To make matters worse, the wind suddenly died down. Boarding parties were hastily prepared on the closest Spanish ships, but they saw eleven longboats drop quickly over the side of the *Ark Royal*. At first they thought the English were cowards and were trying to escape, abandoning their ship without a fight; instead the English took the large galleon in tow and moved her away. As she was towed past the *San Martín*, the two rival flagships exchanged a few broadsides, climaxed by the duke's order to lower longboats also, not to attack the enemy but to tow away his own galleon, which was getting the worst of the exchange.

The wind came up again by the time the *Ark Royal* was out of the center of the Armada, her sails quickly filled, and she left the astonished Spaniards believing that Saint Dominic was actually siding with the English heretics instead of with them. Howard rejoined the seaward division of his fleet which began their terrible cannonading again, while Drake and Hawkins led the landward division in a furious rush at the other flank of the Armada, forcing it to give up the plan of cornering them against the shore. The thousands of spectators on the beaches and in small boats could hardly complain of boredom that day. Hours went by as the combined English fleet hovered around the Armada on three sides, continuously pounding the Spaniards with heavy cannon fire. By midafternoon many of the Spanish ships had used the last of their powder supply and could not even return the fire.

By that time the Armada was approaching the eastern end of the Isle of Wight and should have been making the tack to enter the Solent, when the duke suddenly ordered the ships to continue on their easterly course toward the French coast, where he believed that Parma was waiting for

Series by Pine showing progress of battles

him with the invasion army. Of all the duke's serious blunders few could equal this one. In the Solent the Armada would have been comparatively safe and could easily have taken the Isle of Wight. There they could have held out either until more powder and supplies reached them from Spain or Flanders, or until the English fleet had been driven away by bad weather. It is true that the English fleet was then pressing hard against his Armada and would certainly have launched their fiercest attack as the Spanish tacked to enter the Solent, but we must consider that, even though the English had already fired over 100,000 cannon balls against the Armada, not one ship had yet been sunk by cannon fire, and it is also certain that the Armada could have sustained the worst the English could offer and still have taken and held the Isle of Wight.

The duke sent his fastest pinnace with another message to Parma, telling him to be prepared to embark his troops in a few days, and begging him to send all the powder and shot possible in haste. Little did the duke realize that Parma had no munitions, and in fact had expected the Armada to bring him all the items he would need for the invasion.

The scarcity of powder and shot was a problem that was to plague both fleets almost equally and determine the course of the battle in so many ways. After the relentless cannonading off the Isle of Wight, both sides were so short of these supplies that the next day passed without one shot being fired. Lord Howard received word from ashore that there was a serious shortage all over England and that almost all the forts and castles had been stripped bare already. This was a crisis not only for the fleet, but also for the shore defenses if Parma's army ever landed.

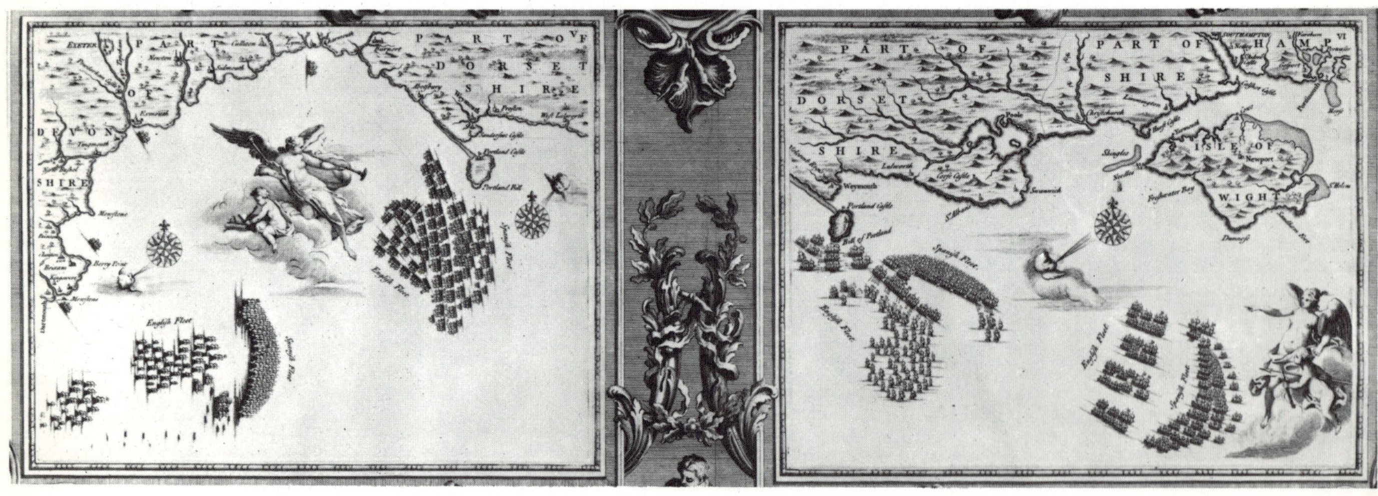

The Spaniards believed that once in French waters the English would give up their pursuit and return to cruise off their own coasts, rather than risk tangling with the French, with whom they were not on very good terms at the time. They also believed that once contact had been made with Parma, and his great army and vast amount of war materials had been embarked on the Armada, the invasion would proceed as planned with little interference from the English, who the Spaniards suspected had already exhausted their munition supplies.

It was with great relief, then, that the coast of France was sighted on the morning of August 6. The news of the fierce sea battle that had been raging in the Channel had already traveled all over Europe, and, as on the English coast, there were also thousands of spectators rushing eagerly along the shore, hoping to catch a glimpse of some action between the two greatest fleets ever assembled. The Duke of Medina Sidonia dispatched another message to Parma, this being his seventh since the Armada had first sighted the English coast, but like all the others it was intercepted by English picket boats, which were blockading the Flemish coast along with a Dutch fleet. Actually Parma had received no word from the Armada since it had left Corunna.

The duke's decision to anchor in Calais that afternoon was not a wise one. It was considered the least sheltered and most dangerous anchorage on that whole coast, and he could not even be certain it was in friendly hands, as events changed nearly daily on the continent. Worst of all, the duke believed that Parma was in Calais, whereas the barge flotilla and army had been assembled in Dunkirk. It seems impossible that the duke

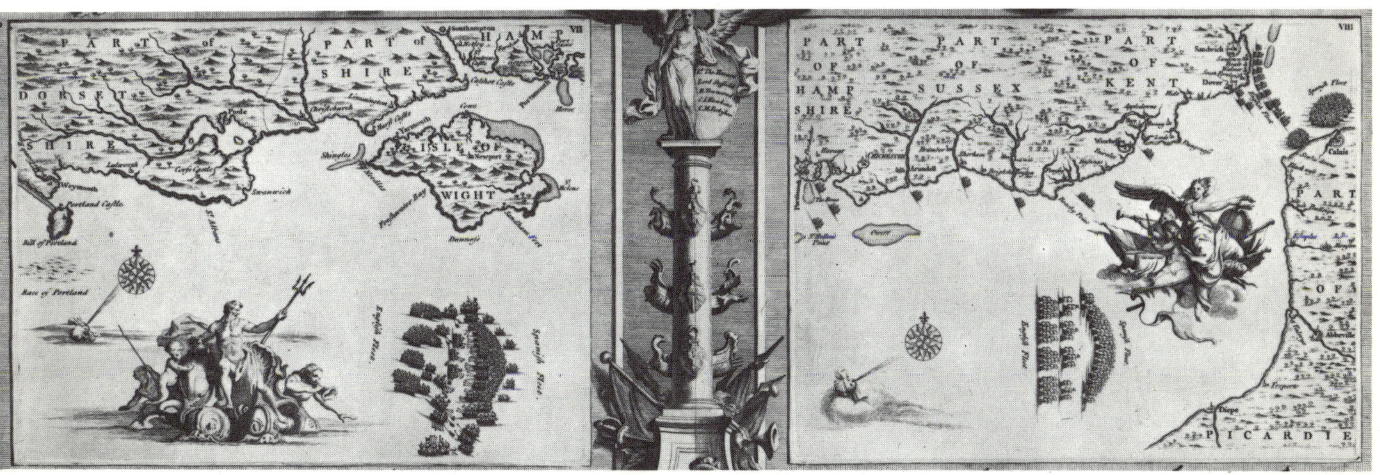

could make such a fundamental mistake, but then one must remember that the king's orders only specified that the Armada should go to the North Foreland, a point of land halfway between Calais and Dunkirk, and there might have been plans that were later canceled for Parma to load part of his army on the Armada ships in Calais. Many believe that the duke decided to enter a French port in hopes that the English would honor French neutrality, and that the Armada would be safer there than in a port held by Parma.

Shortly after both fleets had anchored, the governor of the port came out and boarded the *San Martín*, expressing great surprise that the Armada had stopped there and warning the duke that a sudden change in wind could drive the whole fleet on the shore. Luckily for the Spaniards, the governor was in the service of the Duke of Guise, the leader of the Catholic forces in France, and he offered them all the port's facilities and freedom to send messages overland to Parma. The duke told the governor that he was sure that Parma was already on his way with his invasion force and by Monday morning they would all be under way heading for the English coast. Believing that the tide of fortune was finally changing in his favor, the duke had the first peaceful night of sleep in a week.

Sunday morning, August 7, officials were sent ashore to buy fresh provisions for the Armada. Many men were sick from scurvy, a disease caused by lack of Vitamin C and remedied in those days by feeding the men an abundant amount of fresh vegetables and fruit, especially citrus fruit. They were also sent to buy powder and shot, but even though high prices were offered, none could be found. Religious services were held on both fleets,

Action against the Dutch

as it was Sunday, but it could not be considered a day of rest, for there was too much urgent work to be done on all the ships, particularly in replacing damaged rigging and masts.

During the morning, while the duke was entertaining friends on the sunlit quarterdeck of his great galleon, he was interrupted by the return of one of the messengers he had sent to Parma the previous evening. The news was staggering. Parma was not even in Dunkirk, but in Bruges, some miles inland, and he wrote that he had already disbanded much of his invasion force to fight the Dutch rebels in various sectors. It was then that the duke first learned that not one of his messages had ever reached Parma. For several weeks Parma had been ready with 16,000 soldiers waiting on barges in Dunkirk and Nieuport, and the remainder prepared to embark on Armada vessels. But only three or four days earlier, about the third or fourth of August, Parma had received word, from what he believed a very reliable source, that the main body of the Armada had been forced to return to Spain, and that the invasion was canceled until the following

91

year. This news induced him to order most of his army to move inland to renew the war against the belligerent Dutch and to destroy most of the barges rather than waste a large force to guard them against enemy attack. Parma went on to say that even when the invasion forces were ready again, which would take several weeks, he still had no intention of leaving port until he was convinced that the Armada could protect it, and this depended on the Armada's first destroying both the English and Dutch fleets in the area.

The duke was so upset by this letter that he accused the messenger of being a spy in the service of the enemy and even had him arrested. He could not believe the news, but two of his own servants sent to find Parma and make sure the letter was not a forgery returned that afternoon with the same information and another letter from Parma. In a very sarcastic tone Parma blamed the duke for all the mishaps, and criticized him particularly for not keeping in close contact as he neared the meeting point. The last, we know, was not the duke's fault, although most of the rest was.

Later in the day the duke received even gloomier news. The French governor demanded that the Spaniards leave the harbor immediately. He felt certain that the English would attack the Armada soon and this would end in trouble for the governor no matter which side won. He especially feared that the English would attempt to capture Calais, which had been lost to the French after centuries in English hands, and they could use the excuse that the French fort had aided the Spaniards in the battle even if it remained neutral and did nothing.

The governor was not far from right. Lord Seymour's Channel Squadron of thirty-six ships had already left its cruising station and joined the rest of the English fleet, which was now much larger than the Armada. Lord Howard hoped that the Spaniards would try to move toward Dunkirk soon, and he preferred to attack them on the high seas rather than in a neutral port, but it was becoming increasingly difficult to restrain his more headstrong officers like Drake, who pressed him to attack the Armada immediately before it could receive more powder and men from Parma.

Around four that afternoon, an English pinnace carrying a light gun suddenly appeared out of the bright glare from the setting sun, ran straight for the *San Martín,* and fired four shots into her hull before one

The Tiger

of the galleasses chased it away. The daring of the men on that small vessel was greatly admired by the Spaniards as well as the English, but it was the first sign that Howard was losing his patience and had decided against honoring the neutrality of the port. Even though he sent word to the governor that the pinnace had acted on its own, neither the French nor the Spanish believed him.

That evening another council of war was held on the *Ark Royal* to sum up the situation. There had been a week of erratic fighting, with the Spaniards getting the worst of it, but the Armada was still intact. The English were unaware that Parma was totally unprepared to embark and that he had no powder and shot of his own, much less enough to send to the Armada. In fact, they feared that the week's fighting had almost been in vain, and that soon the invasion of England would be under way. Causing them even more worry was the state of their provisions, which were down to almost nothing on most ships. Some food could possibly be obtained, but Parma might join the Armada in the meantime. Then there was the biggest problem of all—the scarcity of powder and shot.

They had barely enough for an hour's battle and there was practically none left in England. Several boats had been sent to the Dutch fleet then cruising off Dunkirk, but these returned with the news that the Dutch were in the same state.

For these reasons, and fearing that bad weather might strike them in their unprotected anchorage near the Armada, all the English leaders decided unanimously that they must act immediately, or everything would be lost. A long-drawn-out battle of broadsides was out of the question because of lack of munitions, nor could they board the enemy ships, because the Spaniards had more soldiers, and even the English admitted that the enemy was much better than they at that type of warfare. This left the much-talked-about but little-used tactic of fireships.

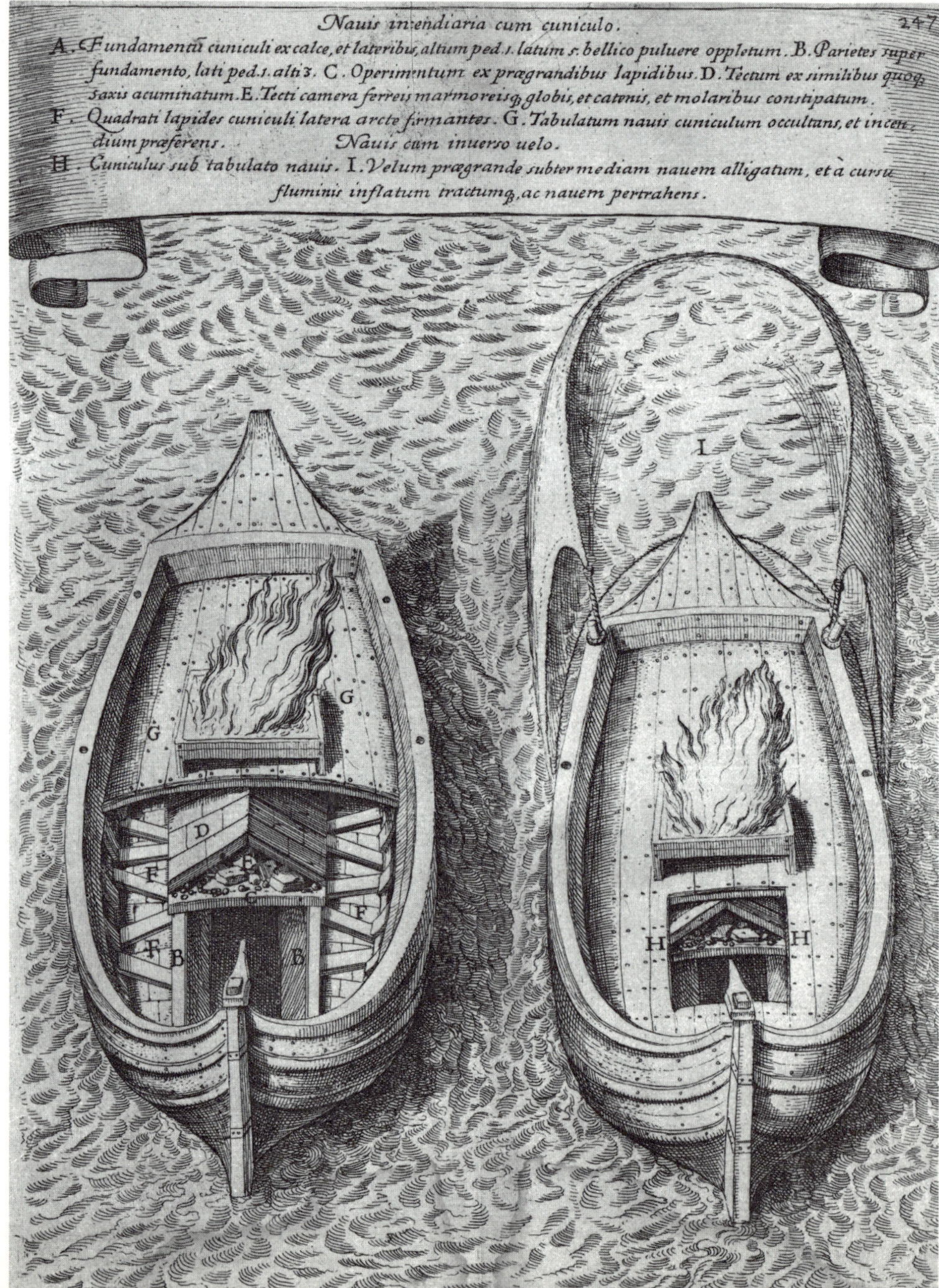

Fireships

The launching of the fireships against the Spanish Armada

Conditions would be ideal that very night. The wind still blew from the west and the incoming tide would be flowing in a direct line from the English fleet to the Armada. The fireships Howard had ordered prepared in Dover for this very purpose had not yet arrived, so eight large hulks were quickly prepared right there. The usual practice was to fill them with powder that would explode on reaching the enemy ships, but since powder was so short, tons of combustible materials were stored in them and each hulk, sails and all, was covered with pitch. Sticking out like porcupine quills from the numerous gun ports, tied to the rigging and attached around the gunwales, were hundreds of flares and rockets that would shoot off as the flames reached them, with the hopes that each one would land on the deck of a Spanish ship, creating fires and confusion.

Everything seemed to be perfect. The sky had a heavy layer of low-lying clouds that obscured the moonlight. Shortly before midnight all eight fireships began creeping quietly toward the anchored Armada. As soon as they were aimed right for the center, they were set ablaze, and their crews jumped quickly aboard skiffs and raced back toward the English fleet. The fireships drifted toward the target, burning more and more brightly the closer they came.

95

The Duke of Medina Sidonia had feared that the English might try this trick and had sent one small pinnace to cruise between both fleets and tow away any fireships before they reached the Armada. How it was expected to handle more than one fireship was never explained, and instead of being even partially useful, the crew fell into such a state of panic when they saw the eight fireships approaching, which they believed were full of powder and would soon explode, that most of them flung themselves into the water.

The panic and horror on the rest of the ships could not have been greater if the Devil had suddenly appeared in person on their decks. Except for the limited number of men on watch, all the rest were asleep, when suddenly it seemed that "the bowels of hell had opened and the end of the world had come," as one of the survivors recorded in his diary. Another wrote that he believed it was raining fire from the skies when all the rockets, flares, and flying objects were thrown from the fireships. Innumerable fires were started all over the Armada, but they caused much more confusion and panic than actual damage.

Fireships off Calais, by Pine

Expecting the incoming tide that night to be a strong one, each ship in the Armada had placed its two heaviest anchors out to keep from dragging toward shore, but this created a serious problem. Since it would have taken about an hour to haul both of them up onto the ships, the duke ordered the anchor cables cut and the Armada to head seaward as quickly as possible. The *San Martín* was in the lead and, passing safely between two of the burning fireships, set a course for another shelter nearby, hoping that the rest of the ships could follow. An hour later she had dropped anchor and the duke believed he had skillfully and successfully eluded the threatening danger, but the main body of the Armada had unfortunately been sent to sea so ill-equipped that in most cases the ships had no third anchor and the few that did had them stored below decks, where they could not be easily reached. Thus over half the Armada just drifted in a disorderly fashion to leeward of the area where the duke was anchored. Astonishing as it seems, not one of the fireships hit a Spanish vessel. After passing right through the middle of the Armada and in many cases actually brushing against a few ships, they finally burned themselves out and sank. Yet they had actually done more damage than the whole English fleet had been able to do in a full week of battle. In the panic of trying to escape, many Spanish vessels collided with one another and sustained serious damages, the countless fires on many of the ships had destroyed many sails and rigging, and worst of all the Armada was badly scattered.

As the sun rose that Monday morning, August 8, the duke's satisfaction turned to anguish when he found only forty other ships of the Armada near him, with the rest already six miles to leeward and very close to the dangerous coast near Dunkirk. Too ignorant to realize the full peril of the situation, he first signaled the scattered remnants of his fleet to rejoin him, but with the wind and current against this plan he then ordered the ships around him to raise anchor and join the others. After a long argument, in which the duke actually struck one of the senior pilots for explaining that these ships might be lost if they sailed to join the others so close to shore, the duke changed the order and said they would simply go seaward and wait for the other vessels to get away from that coast into deeper water.

Ashore, the spectacle was equally disheartening. One of the galleasses, in trying to escape from the path of the fireships the night before, had

Spanish ships burning

caught an anchor cable from another ship in its rudder and could not be steered. The galley slaves, many of whom were English and Dutch, took the opportunity to rebel at that moment, so that the oars could not be used either for steering or propulsion. Before the slaves could be brought back into submission, the galleass was driven ashore by the incoming tide and was left high on the beach when the tide flowed out again, lying over on her side in such a way that none of her cannon could be fired. She then became the helpless target of an attack by the crews of six English ships, including the *Ark Royal*, who landed in longboats.

The garrison of the French fort had no intention of provoking the English, so they did nothing but watch from the high walls of the fort and hope that the English would not decide to attack them also. The Spanish admiral on the galleass and his men put up a gallant defense, holding the attackers off for over three hours, but when the admiral was finally killed by a musket ball, the surviving sailors and soldiers gave up all hope. They jumped onto the beach and ran for the town, with some of the English chasing them right into the main square, brandishing cutlasses and pistols and scattering the astonished townsfolk. The galleass was taken and plundered, and after releasing the galley slaves the English began trying to refloat her.

At this time the French fort commander decided he had suffered enough humiliation from the English, so he fired a warning cannon shot over their heads and sent a message ordering them to leave the beach and the galleass, which he claimed as the property of the French king. This defiant act so enraged Lord Howard that instead of rushing out to join Drake and the rest of his fleet, he spent most of the day arguing with the French over the ownership of the already worthless galleass.

This was the day that would decide the future of Europe, the day in which the Protestants, if victorious, would be forever safe from Catholic aggression, and the day in which the English might strip Spain of the supremacy of the seas. Drake and Hawkins knew that it was England's last chance. If the scattered Armada ships ever regrouped and obtained more supplies, the tide of battle would probably turn in their favor. Astonished that Howard was wasting his time disputing a single prize, they took the initiative and rallied the rest of the English fleet around them.

The Duke of Medina Sidonia, not really knowing which way to turn, had wasted over an hour in deciding what action to take. The forty ships with him were finally in the process of hauling up their anchors to head seaward when the English fleet led by Drake and Hawkins, which out-numbered them by over three to one, suddenly appeared out of the dense fog, hoping to deal the decisive blow. Again the duke had to order many of the anchor cables cut, and fully aware that even with full sail on they could not outrun the faster English ships, he ordered them all to turn about, point their bows into the wind, and meet their attackers head-on. The duke was lucky that most of the forty ships with him were the best in the whole Armada, with the great admirals Recalde, de Leyva, Oquendo, and Bertendona commanding them.

The first burst of the English storm fell on the *San Martín*, sandwiched between the ships of Drake and Hawkins. Because of their shortage of munitions, every shot had to count, and English ships sailed so close to the Spanish before each broadside that a few Spanish boarders were actually able to swing from the rigging over onto the English ships, although they were quickly overcome by the English crews. Soon the smoke from the cannon and fires that had started on several ships was so thick that in a few cases ships of the same side were firing on one another. Neither the Spanish nor English admiral could give orders to his flock, so each captain had to act as he saw fit. Because it was fought at such close range, this battle was much fiercer and bloodier than any of the others.

At one time, shortly after the fighting had started, there were seventeen English ships engaged in cannonading the *San Martín*. The duke, who only a week before had never heard a shot fired in anger, was so frightened

Capture and burning of the San Salvador

that he deserted his post, placing one of the pilots in charge, and retired to his cabin, which had been lined on all sides with large bales of wool to stop any shot from bursting through the walls. He flung himself on the deck of his cabin and lay there for hours crying and praying. Later he was justly accused of cowardice, and only his high social position saved him from the execution he deserved.

Although the *San Martín's* timbers were of double thickness, many of the cannon balls fired at such close range went right through her hull, and she took on a great deal of water through many of these holes. Her decks, like those on many other Spanish ships, were a slaughterhouse, with nearly three fourths of the men dead or wounded. She was slowly sinking when Oquendo and de Leyva dashed in with their galleons and forced the English to turn all their fire on them, while other ships quickly moved in to pull the ailing *San Martín* away and make emergency repairs.

The rest of the Spaniards also distinguished themselves with desperate heroism. The battle lasted longer than the English leaders had expected, for shortly after the fighting started several English ships had arrived with additional stores of powder sent from the Dutch for the fight against their common enemy, Spain. As the battle continued, with the Spaniards receiving most of the blows, many of the English captains offered surrender terms, only to be answered by more furious fighting from the brave Spaniards. Not one ship struck its colors—the indication that a ship wanted to surrender. Blood was seen streaming off the decks of most Spanish ships, and priests knelt administering the last rites to dying men, even during the hottest fighting. The Spaniards for the most part had completely exhausted their powder by noon, but they refused to yield and withstood one broadside after another without being able to answer the fire. The main body of the Armada, which that morning had been dangerously close to shore, had all managed to free themselves from those shallow waters, but they could not reach the combat areas and come to the aid of their companions as both wind and current were too strong against them.

Late in the afternoon, when most of the English ships were out of ammunition again, a very strong squall struck, causing the remaining English ships to cease their fire and attend to weathering the storm. While the English turned about and took the necessary precaution of facing into the wind, the Spanish vessels, too badly battered to maneuver, were

The Invincible Armada, by Visscher

pushed to leeward at a reckless speed. When the squall finally abated after an hour, both forces were finally separated, and the English decided not to close the gap and resume the battle as they were once again out of powder.

In the smoke of the battle and then in the heavy rainfall which accompanied the squall, neither side had been able to see the full extent of damage the once great Armada had suffered. With the air now clear and dry, the sight was as horrifying to the Spanish as it was welcome to the English. One of Recalde's galleons had sunk during the squall, with a total loss of life. Two others from the duke's own squadron had been demasted while trying to aid the *San Martín* during the battle and were driven toward the rebel-held coast, where later that night both wrecked and the few survivors were captured and beheaded by the Dutch. The condition of the rest of the ships was little better. Many of them barely had crews left, for the number of Spaniards killed since the first battle off Plymouth was now over 10,000. Thousands of sailors and soldiers

102

were seen floating in the bloodstained seas, and thousands more were piled up on the decks of the ships awaiting a more decent sea burial when time permitted. Most ships were so badly crippled that they could barely sail and unless they could be quickly repaired most of them were expected to sink. Most of the Spanish officers admitted later that if the English had been able to continue their attack for a few more hours they could have destroyed every one of the Armada's ships.

By sunset the battered remnants of this Armada had already been swept well past Dunkirk, which was not only the last friendly port but also the last chance of joining with Parma's invasion force. But even if they had been able to enter Dunkirk, most leaders on both sides agreed that no invasion could have taken place that year, and if one were to be made the following year, a completely new Armada would be necessary.

The Duke of Medina Sidonia was finally calmed down by his personal chaplain and summoned the courage to leave his cabin to appear on the quarterdeck, having aged at least ten years from the day's ordeal. He tried feebly to take command again but by then there was little even a good leader could do. Repairs were going on as best they could and in several cases three ships would be seen side by side, the outer two holding up the middle one lest she sink before her leaks could be plugged.

The English were also very busy making repairs, but their damages were not half as serious as those they had dealt the Spanish. Meanwhile Howard had finally rejoined his fleet after wasting the whole day trying to refloat the galleass, which he had failed to do even after the fort commander had finally given his permission. Drake had already sent dozens of his fastest boats to carry the wounded to England and obtain more powder, as he hoped to renew the battle the following morning at first light. On many of his ships the plight of the crews was very serious, not so much from the actual combat but from hunger and thirst. On several ships it was reported that all the food and water had been consumed three days earlier and the men were keeping alive by eating rats and catching what little rain water they could.

The night passed miserably for the Spaniards. No one could sleep because it was a race against time to keep most of the ships from sinking. Most of the small supply of food and water that remained had to be cast overboard to help the sinking ships stay afloat. Many ships had to push all their cannon, which were the heaviest items, into the water also, but the men did not consider this as great a loss as the food and water, as they had no ammunition and little chance of obtaining any. There were also several hundred horses and mules brought along for Parma's army, but these too had to be thrown overboard. There was no more fodder left for them, so they would have died from starvation anyway.

Sometime during the night the undamaged part of the Armada was able to rejoin the rest of the fleet, and men and supplies were quickly transferred to the worst-hit vessels. At dawn on Tuesday, August 9, the whole Armada was making its way into the North Sea with the wind, now reaching gale force, driving it east toward some very treacherous shoals. The duke's ship, which had been repaired with many items stripped off other vessels, was able to tack to windward away from the danger, but only a few others were able to follow, either because they were too badly damaged or because most Spanish ships were simply bad sailors.

The English fleet hung off about a mile away, gleefully watching the fate that awaited the Armada. Great foaming breakers were flying all over the shoals, and the water was becoming very shallow with many ships already scraping bottom, expecting the end at any moment. But good fortune finally fell on the hapless Armada. The wind direction suddenly shifted to west-southwest, enabling the whole fleet to make deeper water. Once they were away from the danger and regrouped, the duke ordered them to head due north up the middle of the North Sea.

Pursuit up the Straits

Later that day the duke called another of his many councils of war to decide on the next course of action. Many of the officers were so badly wounded or so angry with the duke that they refused to attend; others came but refused to join in the discussions. Discouraged by the horrifying defeat they had suffered under the duke's incompetent leadership, they were still too proud to admit that there was only one solution left—give up and go home. A few hotheads were for renewing the battle even at the risk of losing every ship and man on board, while others advocated entering a neutral port in Norway to spend the winter and refit for another invasion attempt the following year.

The duke barely opened his mouth, but Oquendo, De Leyva and a few other experienced officers took command of the meeting. They explained that even though two thirds of the Armada's ships were in fair condition, having been spared the previous day's battle, almost all these were only transports or small pinnaces and sloops, while none of the fighting ships could possibly withstand another battle even if there had been any powder and shot left. Thus the entire Armada would undoubtedly be destroyed in another battle. They ruled out the idea of wintering in Norway or anywhere else, because the coasts of Spain would be left undefended for a long period, they would need great amounts of money to buy supplies for the surviving men without much hope that the king would send them any after their miserable defeat. This left them with only one choice, that of admitting defeat and returning to Spain with what was left of the Armada. They would at least have the nucleus with which to build another fleet; then they could return to defeat the English so soundly that the whole world would know that Spanish honor was restored.

After much arguing this plan was accepted. Since the wind was blowing continuously from the west, and the English fleet, which would probably be reinforced soon by a Dutch fleet, was between them and the entrance to the English Channel, they had no choice but to continue sailing north, pass around Scotland and down the western side of Ireland, and then set a straight course for Spain. A long hard journey was still ahead, and many must have thought it would be better to perish in those cold, unfriendly waters than face the anger of their king and the scorn of their countrymen when the once proud Armada, the hope of all Catholic Europe, reached home in defeat.

V

Humiliated, hungry, thirsty, and losing many men daily from their recent wounds, the Spaniards sailed northward, propelled by brisk southwesterly winds and with the English still close behind. Lord Howard and his officers had decided that the immediate danger of an invasion was over, but they still had no inkling that Parma's army had been disbanded nor did they realize the full extent of the Armada's damages. They had so little powder left themselves that any battle was out of the question, but they decided to shadow the Armada until there was no longer any possibility of its turning south again and threatening England's shores. One day they were almost able to capture Recalde's disabled galleon, which had lagged behind once again, but without powder they were powerless to interfere with the pinnaces sent back to tow the ship to safety out of their reach.

Many of the English leaders believed that the Spaniards had not given up entirely and that they still might try something else. They could have entered a Scottish port, for one thing, where they would have received a warm welcome from the Catholics, who were still very angry with Elizabeth for executing Mary Stuart and many of whom wished to invade England from the north with the aid of the Armada.

It seems strange that the Spaniards never even considered stopping in a Scottish port for repairs or at least sending in a few ships to obtain supplies, when they were perfectly aware that many Scots favored their cause. Perhaps they were so ashamed of their disgraceful defeat that pride compelled them to try to reach home with what means were at hand.

On Friday, August 12, the Armada passed the mouth of the Firth of Forth, about sixty miles off shore, and the wind then changed to northwest. By then Howard was convinced that the Armada was only intent on fleeing back to Spain, and he ordered the English fleet to abandon their pursuit and return to home port, leaving only two small swift ships to stay with the Armada and report any change in course or suspicious activities.

Turning back, the English ran right into the center of a strong westerly gale, which scattered them, but eventually they all limped safely into various ports of England. The state of their fleet by that time was nearly as bad as that of the Armada, and they would have had to break off their chase and return home in any case, as Elizabeth had sent them neither powder nor provisions and they were in no condition to prevent the Spaniards from rejoining Parma or doing anything else they pleased.

Relieved of the alarming presence of the English fleet, the Spaniards were now able to devote more of their time and energy to surveying their condition and preparing for a voyage that might take a month or more. Even in normal conditions a voyage up to the Orkneys and around Ireland was very long and dangerous. In view of the terrible state of the Spanish ships and crews, as well as the lack of good pilots or charts of those waters, the Spaniards had much cause for worry. On many of the ships there were so few seamen left that soldiers and even gentlemen

Commencement of the flight north

volunteers had quickly to learn the ways of the sea and take over the shipboard duties, such as setting the sails. The daily rations for each man were reduced to a half pound of moldy, vermin-infested biscuit, a pint of foul-smelling water and a half pint of wine, which in most cases had already turned to vinegar. The poor men had been improperly clothed from the start of the expedition and many had had to use their own clothes as bandages for their wounded comrades and themselves, so that by this time most were nearly nude, and each day they proceeded farther north the temperatures fell lower and lower, adding even more to their misery. Over a third of the men had already died from injuries and wounds suffered in battle, and of the remainder the majority were casualties either from the battles or from various illnesses such as scurvy or typhus, with the number of this latter group increasing daily.

After the English fleet had separated from the Armada, the duke had shut himself in his cabin. He rarely left it, and he spoke with no one on the whole voyage back to Spain. Vice-admiral Diego de Valdez became the practicing commander of the Armada, and this made the men somewhat happier, if men in such desperate straits could be happy. If the duke ever sympathized with the men's distress, he did not show it. Fully aware that he was the person most responsible for the stunning defeat they had suffered and that nearly every soul in the Armada distrusted and despised him, he only added to their already great resentment by keeping aloof, unwilling to share the hardships with them.

Yet it pleased the duke, while secluded in his cabin, to order an inquiry into the conduct of the commanders of all Armada vessels that had been unable to fight in the bloody battle of Gravelines on August 8, because they had been blown to leeward and the wind and current had prevented them from rejoining those forty galleons that had withstood the English onslaught with the duke's own flagship. The officers appointed by the duke to hold the inquiry completely acquitted all the accused, but the duke then accused them of cowardice—a remarkable charge, considering that he himself was considered by most of the men one of the worst cowards ever to have fought under the Spanish flag. He presided personally over a court-martial and ordered that twenty of the captains be executed. Then, fearing a general mutiny of the whole Armada, he commuted their sentence to imprisonment, except in the case of two poor officers, captains Cuellar and Cristobal de Avila, who he claimed were

The route of the Spanish Armada

guilty not only of the same charge against the other captains of refusing to join in the battle with the rest of the Armada, but also of deserting the *San Martín* in an earlier battle and leaving it to face the enemy alone. Everyone knew that both charges were completely untrue, but there was little anyone could do.

Captain Avila, to the disgust of everyone, was executed that same day. He was hanged from the yardarm of a pinnace, which was then sent around the whole Armada with the unfortunate man's body dangling there for all to see. This act so thoroughly angered the men that if it had not been for their weak condition, many believed they would have mutinied and given the duke the same treatment he had ordered for the innocent captain. Captain Cuellar was to suffer the same fate the following day, but when the duke learned how the men had reacted to Captain Avila's execution, he changed the death sentence and had him imprisoned like the rest of the other ships' commanders.

In an age when news traveled slowly and usually became more and more distorted the farther it was carried, rumors took over from fact after that last fierce battle at Gravelines near Calais. Even a week after the battle had been fought and lost by the Spaniards, King Philip believed that the Armada had been triumphant, that Parma had already landed his army on English soil and was making good progress with the conquest of England. On August 18 he wrote the Duke of Medina Sidonia a long letter congratulating him on his victory, which the king said he had learned about from an eyewitness who also had claimed that the Armada had sunk forty English ships in battle, captured thirty others, and that Drake, Spain's archenemy, had been killed in battle. The king not only ordered every church in Spain to offer masses in thanksgiving for the success of the Armada, but also quickly dispatched a special ambassador to Rome to demand from the Pope the one million crowns he had promised Philip the moment he learned that Parma's army was actually ashore and fighting on English soil.

By the end of August, however, the horrid truth finally reached Spain and their joy turned to sadness. The Duke of Medina Sidonia, in compliance with a royal order received at Calais, wrote to Philip as often as he could to report the state of affairs, but only two of these letters, both giving the king a vivid picture of the terrible miseries the Armada was suffering, ever reached the king. For weeks the king, praying and hoping that by some chance it could still unite with Parma and launch the invasion, refused to believe that his Invincible Armada had failed. It was not until the end of September, when he received a letter from the duke written from Santander in Spain announcing his arrival in that port, that Philip finally admitted that the expedition had been a complete failure.

Meanwhile the English fleet had returned victorious to its home ports, but their victory was somewhat spoiled by the fear that the Spaniards might still have some scheme, perhaps to stir up and unite with the Scottish Catholics or the Irish rebels. With the fleet disbanded under the queen's orders, there would be nothing to stop them. Although never wavering in their loyalty to their queen, many of the leaders were becoming very critical of her method of conducting the war. They had defeated the Armada, it was true, but many believed justly that this had

Queen Elizabeth
giving thanks for deliverance

been accomplished by good luck and in spite of the queen, who had always failed to provide enough supplies and munitions. Now once again it seemed to them that she was more interested in saving money than in saving her kingdom.

When the news first reached London at the end of July that the Armada had been sighted off the southwest coast of England, Elizabeth had rushed quickly into action. After issuing hundreds of orders regarding the defense of the nation, she went to visit and inspect many of the recently established army camps set up along the coasts, vowing that she would lead her loyal subjects to victory even if she herself had to fight in the muddy ditches with the common soldiers. Yet no sooner had the peril passed than she once again turned to thoughts of economy. Without even waiting to hear whether the Armada had entered the Firth of Forth to join the Scottish Catholics or not, as many of her closest advisers feared it might do, she ordered her armies disbanded and the men sent home.

When the fleet reached their home ports, orders were waiting that the ships were to be laid up and the crews dismissed, even though there was still some danger that the Armada might return. Lord Howard was ordered to rush to London and present himself to the queen, which he and everyone else expected was in order to receive some honor for the great victory. Instead she had summoned him only in order that he might attend to all the details of demobilizing the fleet under her watchful eyes,

*Queen Elizabeth riding in triumph
through London*

so that she could be sure not a shilling was wasted. Howard even found
that Elizabeth would neither give the necessary funds to pay the poor
men their usual wages nor even repay Drake, Hawkins, and many others
like himself who had spent their own money in buying last-minute supplies for the fleet. Thus with the exception of the few lucky men who
had collected prize money from the galleon captured by Drake, and then
only because Drake had divided up the booty before the queen's orders
to turn it all over to her had arrived, none of the thousands of brave
Englishmen who had endured such sufferings and hardships for queen
and country ever received the reward due them.

The English people were slow to react to the victory, mainly because
they had heard so many contradictory and false rumors. Not until the
queen herself announced the good news in a special session of Parliament
did the majority of the populace believe it. Londoners showed their gratitude by staging a series of lavish celebrations, but it was not until Sunday,
November 24, that the queen joined in the festivities. Attended by her
privy council and most of the nobility of the realm and all the leaders of
the fleet, all riding splendid horses or carried in richly decorated coaches,
the queen rode in a beautiful chariot drawn by two white horses, leading
them all to Saint Paul's Cathedral. Upon entering the great west door,
she fell on her knees and audibly praised God for her own and the nation's
deliverance from the enemy. All over England the day was proclaimed a

112

Armada medal

national holiday and great festivities were held in every town, lasting well over a week in some cases.

The Armada, plowing into the colder northern waters, managed to stay intact until after reaching the Orkneys. The general plan was that they would continue on their northerly course until reaching the sixtieth parallel, then turn westward and weather their way around the Irish coast. However, shortly after passing the Orkneys the Armada was struck by a gale which scattered the ships, over half of which never rejoined the main body again. Part of the reason was the mist, fog, and short amount of daylight in those northern regions, which prevented them from sighting the other ships, but in many cases the discontented captains welcomed the opportunity to break away from the disastrous leadership of the Duke of Medina Sidonia and shift for themselves. Two or three of the ships were blown as far north as the Faroe Islands and the men suffered terribly from the cold and ice. Other ships formed in small groups of six, eight, or ten, making as much headway as they could, working westward against wind and current, the men dying at an alarming rate.

When they began heading south down the Irish coast, the duke's *San Martín* and sixty other ships that had managed to stay together during the gale steered their course far out into the Atlantic to reduce the danger of being dashed on those shores by a storm, but the other, smaller groups were in too much of a hurry to take this wise precaution and many were

113

lost. So rough were the seas when the main body of the Armada began its southerly descent that not even the mast tops were dry. On August 21 the duke wrote to the king that they were 200 miles west of the Irish coast and believed that unless good fortune soon came their way they would all very shortly be swallowed up by the sea.

Of the smaller groups of ships that had separated from the main body, some were wrecked on the Shetland Islands and others met a similar fate all over the coasts of Scotland and Ireland. Some tried to head for Flanders by taking a short cut south between the east coast of Ireland and west coasts of Scotland and England, but every one of those unfortunate ships was also wrecked. One of these was a galleon on which Admiral Alonzo de Leyva had foundered, and only he and a few nobles were rescued out of the icy water by a galleass. This ship had also suffered a great deal of damage during the gale and over 90 per cent of her galley slaves had perished, leaving her with only sails for power. After a while, as more and more men died or fell too ill to work the ship, they were finally forced to seek the nearest shelter, the Irish port of Killybegs, where they received a friendly welcome from the Ulster chief, O'Donnell. He not only gave them the hospitality of his castle, where the admiral and all the nobles spent a month recovering their health while the crew did likewise and repaired the galleass, but even supplied them with a large amount of money to purchase everything needed for the vessel so that they could at least reach a friendly Flemish port and from there make their way back to Spain. Shortly after leaving, however, bad weather struck and drove them upon some rocks on the Scottish coast, where the vessel was dashed to pieces and everyone aboard was drowned.

Thirty or forty other ships, with their men suffering fearfully from starvation and thirst, were tempted to land on the Irish coast. There were Irishmen serving on many of the ships, who must have convinced their shipmates that they would receive a good welcome from the friendly Irish Catholics, and one ship after another turned toward land. One by one nearly all were driven on the rocky shores of Ireland between Donegal and the Blaskets.

Something like 8000 half-drowned wretches struggled ashore alive, but they found an even more miserable fate awaiting them than they had already suffered. The gentlemen and officers of the ships, soiled and battered as they were, still carried ashore such ornaments and money as

Plunder washed ashore from the wrecks of Spanish ships

they possessed, besides wearing priceless silk and velvet clothing. The common seamen and soldiers had all been paid in Corunna on the morning the Armada had sailed, and because they had never had the opportunity of spending it, splashed ashore with their pockets full of money.

The wild Irish of that coast, many of whom had barely enough to eat themselves, were tempted by the plunder, and, forgetting that these poor men were their allies and of their own religion, bashed countless numbers of Spaniards, and even the Irishmen with them, on the head with their clubs and then stripped them bare of clothes and money, leaving them to die in the cold. On one strip of sandy beach near Sligo, an English officer counted over 1100 bodies, and similar reports were also sent to London by officers in other areas where other massacres took place. The moment many of the more intelligent Irish chiefs heard that a vessel had been wrecked, they would rush down to the shores to prevent their countrymen from disgracing themselves further, saving many unfortunate victims and rushing them to the safety of their castles before they met another horrible fate at the hands of the English.

Along many sections of the Irish coast the forts and castles were garrisoned with English troops to keep the Irish from rebelling. Although they certainly had nothing to fear from the Spaniards at the time, most of whom were unarmed and half dead anyway, they were afraid that if permitted to recover and find shelter among the rebels, they could become extremely dangerous, so the English officers ordered every one of them executed. Over 3000 were captured and hung or shot the first week alone, with the exception of two high-ranking officers who were held for ransom.

The sixty ships with the *San Martín* were able to double around Kerry Head on the west coast of Ireland, after strong westerly winds had driven them dangerously close to the rocky shore, but they were all in a condition scarcely less miserable than that of their companions who at least had met a swift death on the Irish shores. Aside from the great number of men who had died in the actual combat, more than half the others had already died from unattended wounds, thirst, and starvation. The small number of survivors were moving skeletons, or in many cases not even moving, more like shadows than living men, with scarcely enough strength left to haul a line or handle the tiller.

While still in sight of Kerry Head, they were struck by a southwest gale. All were scattered, many never sighting the other ships until they reached home ports, many never reaching port at all.

Admiral Recalde had managed somehow to keep his wrecked hulk afloat by the superhuman efforts of his brave crew. After this last gale subsided, he found that only two other Armada ships were in sight, and all three were very close to shore with their men dying of thirst. Eight years before, Recalde had sailed in those same waters, carrying 1000 Papal troops to aid the Irish rebels in a war against the English. Feeling certain that he would still be remembered and liked by the local inhabitants, he ordered all three ships to head for a small fishing village where he had put those soldiers ashore. Before arriving, one of the other galleons suddenly sank with a total loss of life after her hull had literally fallen apart. The other two galleons entered the harbor and sent boats quickly ashore for the precious water. The local people were so afraid of punishment from the English for aiding the Spaniards that they refused to permit them to land until Recalde himself went ashore and begged them. Finally the Spaniards were permitted to fill their water casks, thus saving the lives of the men for the moment, although most died before ever reaching Spain. On the way home and almost within sight of the Spanish coast, the other galleon foundered one night and not one person survived. A few days later Recalde brought his own ship into Corunna where it sank shortly after the survivors were carried ashore, and there Recalde himself died two days later, probably from shame and grief as much as anything.

Admiral Oquendo also reached Spain alive, only to die a few days later, unwilling to outlive the disgrace of the gallant navy he had so often led to victory in the past.

As the *San Martín* and other scattered Armada vessels dropped down into the warmer latitudes, the weather fortunately became milder, or possibly not one ship would have reached Spain. From the second week of September onward, ships began limping into various ports of northern Spain, many of these sinking right in the harbors before anything could be done to repair them.

On September 22, the *San Martín* crept into the port of Santander, soon followed by eleven other Armada ships that had joined it after the last storm. A few days earlier they had all been off Corunna and had signaled for help, mainly for small boats to tow them into port because they were unable to work their way in against an outflowing tide, but no help was sent, and they just drifted along the coast until reaching Santander where the conditions were more favorable for entering port.

In some ships there had not been a drop of water for over two weeks, and on the *San Martín* alone over 180 men had died of thirst and hunger just in the few weeks since they had last seen the coast of Ireland. The rest of the miserable survivors were all down with fever and there were barely twenty men left on the *San Martín* capable of lowering the anchors.

After the suffering they had all endured, their ordeal was finally over and now they had the warmth of the Spanish sun on their thin, bruised bodies, fresh bread and fruit to eat, and fresh clear water to drink. But, surprisingly, many did not recover, mainly because for the first few weeks all the men were forbidden to come ashore, as the local officials feared they might spread some epidemic. In most cases the dead were not even taken ashore for burial, but lay decaying right in front of the living, so that there is little wonder the others did not regain their health. As soon as the *San Martín* arrived, however, the duke immediately ordered everyone brought ashore in Santander and all the other ports where Armada ships were anchored. But men still continued to die by the hundreds each day, as if some cruel fate were determined to rid the earth of every remnant of that unlucky expedition, while the person most at fault for the failure, the Duke of Medina Sidonia, escaped unharmed.

After the *San Martín* anchored, the duke was rowed ashore where thousands of furious people, many of whom had lost relatives in the disaster, were waiting to shout insults and hurl stones at him. The whole country was against the duke, demanding that he pay with his life for the loss of their hopes and families. Once in the safety of the governor's palace, the duke demanded the punishment of these people for the outrage committed against him, but the local police refused to comply with his order for fear of their own lives at the hands of the mob, which was even then flinging stones at the governor's house. The duke spent hours defending himself before the local officials, who cared nothing about his excuses but were only interested in getting him safely out of their town before he was killed and they were held responsible by the king.

The following day the duke wrote to King Philip reporting briefly what had occurred since his last letter but devoting most of the letter to defending himself against the charge of failing in his duty and demanding troops to guard his life and permission to return as soon as possible to his palace in Sanlúcar in southern Spain. In a postscript he also mentioned briefly the plight of the men on the Armada ships that had made port already and begged the king to do something to ease their suffering.

By that time sixty or sixty-five of the ships had reached various ports in Spain, and except for one or two others still making their way, they were all that was left of the whole Armada, which only a few months before had numbered 130. Besides those that sank after entering port, most were so badly damaged and rotting away that only a few were ever repaired and restored to service in the navy. Of the total number of men who had sailed from Corunna in July, less than one third ever reached Spain alive, and as the majority of these died in port, by the end of the year there were not over three or four thousand men left from the original number of almost 30,000, even counting the few hiding out in Ireland.

On September 27, without even waiting for an answer to his first letter, the impatient duke again wrote the king, insisting that he be permitted to start his journey home and be relieved of the title of Lord High Admiral of the Spanish Navy, as he did not deserve nor want the title. He wrote that he hated ships and everything about the sea so bitterly that even if he ever recovered his health he would never step aboard another ship, even to receive a million-ducat gift. He even claimed that he would prefer to be beheaded as a traitor than ever have anything to do with naval affairs again.

Philip's reaction was very different from what everyone, especially the duke, had expected. He replied in a very affectionate letter telling the

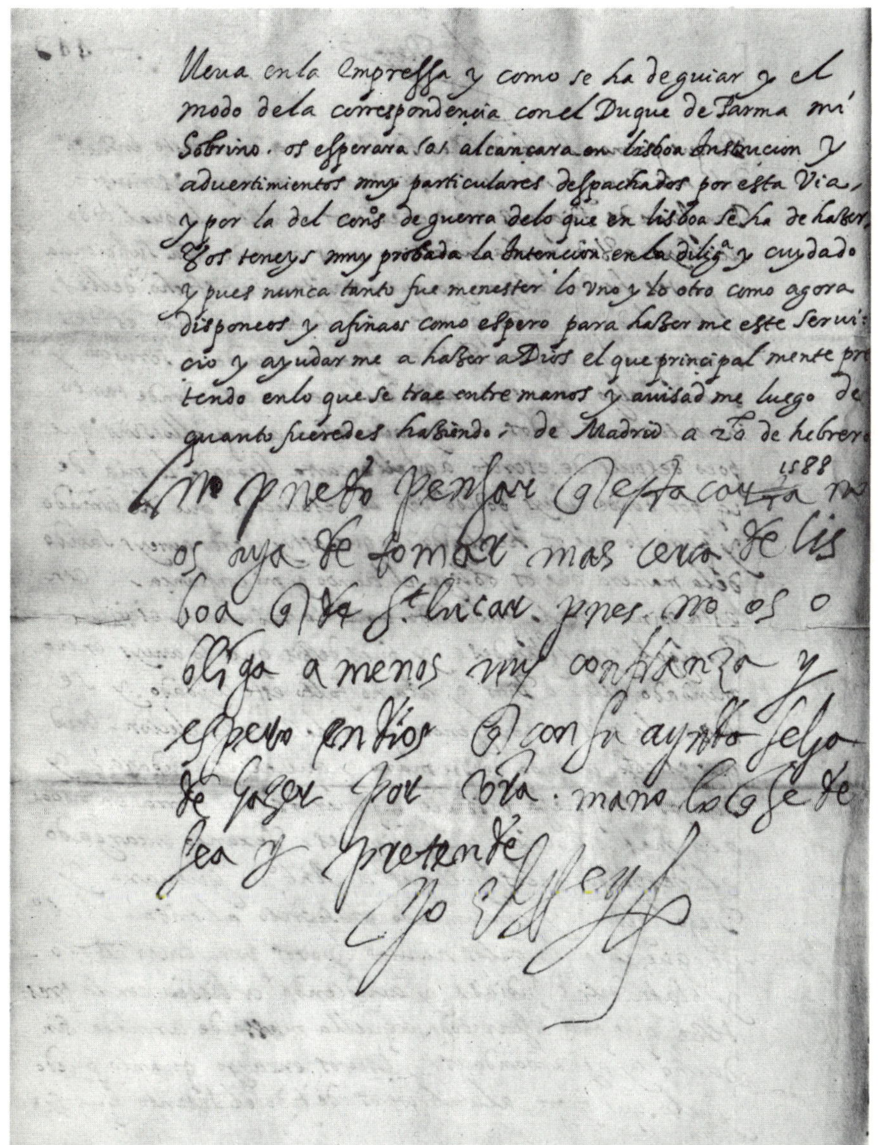

*King Philip's letter
to the defeated Spanish admiral*

duke that in all fairness he could not blame him for the way things had turned out, since he never wanted the responsibility of commanding the Armada in the first place and had only done so at the king's orders. He thanked him for having done what little he could, and even gave him permission to leave for home at the earliest opportunity. Since a scapegoat was needed, the king ordered poor Admiral Diego de Valdez arrested and imprisoned in the Castle of Burgos. There was not really anyone left to blame the disaster on, since the king had cleared the duke and every other Spanish admiral had either been killed in battle, drowned in a shipwreck, or had died shortly after reaching home like Recalde and Oquendo.

Unlike Queen Elizabeth, who had left her gallant seamen to die in the streets for want of victuals and medical treatment after having saved England from invasion, Philip ordered clothes, medicine and everything necessary to be rushed to the survivors—a very noble deed, considering that they had been soundly defeated and Philip was almost bankrupt from the venture. Even the widows and orphans of the Armada's dead soldiers and sailors were sought out later and given state pensions.

The very same day that the Duke of Medina Sidonia received the king's permission to abandon his post and head for home, he stole away from the town at night and began the long and dangerous journey overland, refusing to go by sea, which would have been a much easier and shorter trip. One would think that after all the harm he had been responsible for directly and indirectly he would at least have been left in obscurity, if not punished. But such was not the case. First the king refused to accept his resignation as Lord High Admiral, and in fact forced him to retain the title for the remaining twenty years of his life, even though the duke kept his vow never to set foot on another ship. The king's action might be explained by a reluctance to admit that he had made a grave mistake in appointing the duke in the first place. But then the king also insisted that the duke retain his post of Captain General of the coasts of Andalusia and Governor of Cádiz, where he had another opportunity of measuring himself against the English seamen, with the same results as before.

In 1596 Lord Essex entered Cádiz harbor as Drake had done in 1587 and not only sank most of the shipping there, but also landed troops and sacked and burned the town. The duke had not developed any soldierly qualities in the meantime but fled from the coast where he lived and rushed to the safety of Seville, on the pretext of seeking reinforcements, and then returned to Cádiz only after every English ship had left for home. Again, instead of being punished for his cowardice, the king named him the supreme councilor for politics and war in 1598, the second highest post in the kingdom, below only those of king and prime minister.

In many ways one cannot help feeling sorry for the Duke of Medina Sidonia, forced to take on responsibilities for which even he admitted he was unfit. But then we must remember that most of the disasters that befell the Armada were a result of his being too proud to listen to good advice from his officers, because he foolishly believed that he could learn everything about commanding a naval force in a matter of weeks, when the rest of the naval officers had taken almost a whole lifetime to learn the same. If more of the responsibility for command had been given to his advisers, the outcome of the venture would no doubt have been much more favorable to Spain.

The defeat of the Spanish Armada was unquestionably the most devastating blow suffered during Philip's long reign—in fact, it was the worst suffered by Spain for many centuries both before and after. It proved that Spain had lost her supremacy of the seas, which by that time she had held for several generations. It was the beginning of the end of the once exclusive monopoly the Spaniards held in the New World, for shortly after this defeat other European nations, especially the English, began to colonize many places in North America and the Caribbean Sea, and English pirates and buccaneers were set loose in large numbers to sack Spanish ports in the Indies and plunder Spanish treasure ships at will, with little interference from the crippled Spanish Navy.

The effect of the Armada's failure was felt most of all in the Netherlands, where Parma's army, idle so long waiting for the invasion of England, began to suffer one defeat after another. The Spaniards captured only one town from the Dutch rebels after the Armada battle, and that was not until forty years later. The war in the Netherlands was to last sixty years after the Armada, but the Dutch slowly milked Spain dry of all her wealth and resources until finally in 1648 they became a free nation, the Holland of today, leaving Spain in such a desperate state that she was no longer considered a major European power.

The English were really modest in their victory, considering the defeat

Sir Francis Drake

of the Armada only a sign of God's favor, without giving credit to their own skill and bravery. Both sides had appealed to God for aid, but He answered the English Protestants. The Catholic nobles and common people of England, who had been waiting for the religious revolution promised by Philip and the Pope that never took place, accepted the verdict of Divine Providence and joined the Anglican Church, which they discovered was not very different from the Catholic Church. The main difference was that that the Anglican Church was a national Church independent of the Pope in Rome, yet now they were able to be loyal to their queen and nation without owing any allegiance to outsiders like the Spaniards. For the first time since Elizabeth's father, King Henry VIII, had broken off relations with Rome, the English became a truly united nation.

Although Philip must have realized that much of the blame for the Armada's defeat lay with him, he too attributed it to "an act of God," and suggested that perhaps the Spaniards had not been sufficiently fervent in their religious devotion. Only a few weeks after he had authorized the Duke of Medina Sidonia to return home, his pen began scratching again preparing new orders for another armada for the same purpose, but this time much larger and closely resembling the original one the Marquis of Santa Cruz had asked for. During the remaining years of his rule he devoted much effort in trying to prepare this new armada, but nothing ever came of it. There were not enough resources left in Spain, and the

whole nation had simply been so discouraged by the defeat of their Invincible Armada that there was little spirit left for a new venture.

If Philip learned in many ways from his defeat, Elizabeth learned almost nothing from her victory, especially the most important lesson,
which was the high cost and the difficulties of trying to invade another
country. Instead she let Drake convince her that the Spaniards should
be given a taste of their own medicine, and she ordered a counterattack
in 1589, by sending an English Armada to invade Portugal and snatch it
away from Philip. She made almost the same mistakes that Philip had
made earlier, even that of placing an inexperienced landsman, Lord Essex,
in command, when Drake or any number of other English sea dogs would
have been a wiser choice. Thus the plan was doomed to failure from the
start. Aside from sacking and destroying Cádiz, in which they obtained
very little booty, nothing was really accomplished, and Elizabeth almost
led her country into poverty and disaster such as Spain had suffered after
the Armada defeat. She continued the war against Spain until her death
in 1603, when peace was finally settled. But no blow England inflicted on
the Spaniards was ever to be as crushing to them as the defeat of their
Invincible Armada.

The author and The World Publishing Company wish to thank the following institutions for the illustrations in this book:

Biblioteca Nacional, Madrid	p. 78
Bodleian Library, Oxford	p. 22
The British Museum	pp. 80, 123
City Art Gallery, Plymouth, England	p. 17
Kunsthistorisches Museum, Vienna	p. 122
The Mansell Collection, London	pp. 13, 19, 35, 38, 71, 82, 86, 94, 113, 115
Musées Royaux des Beaux-Arts, Brussels	p. 25
Museo Naval, Madrid	pp. 20, 48, 67, 77
Museo del Prado, Madrid	pp. 12, 41
The Vatican Museum	p. 14
The National Maritime Museum, Greenwich, England	all other illustrations

INDEX

ABOUT THE AUTHOR

ROBERT F. MARX's zest for naval adventure and history led him to a special fondness for the days of the great sailing ships. Derring-do comes naturally to Mr. Marx, who in 1962, on a replica of Christopher Columbus' ship the *Niña*, followed the earlier explorer's sea route to America, a voyage he described in his book *Following Columbus*. In the spring of 1964, Robert Marx was the captain of a replica of a tenth-century Viking ship, in which he was going to duplicate a Viking voyage to America. After sailing twelve hundred miles, however, the ship was wrecked on the African coast.

When not diving for sunken treasure or embarked on a voyage of exploration, he lives in London with his wife, a scholar who shares his interest in historical research. Formerly on the staff of a large magazine in the United States, he has spent most of the last six years doing historical research in the archives of Europe. Mr. Marx knows how to kindle in his readers the same enthusiasm for the drama of historical events that he himself feels.

More recently he has been reliving the adventures of Robinson Crusoe on the very island where the real-life Crusoe was actually shipwrecked.